High-Yield Orthopaedics
OITE & ABOS Review for Orthopaedic Providers

© 2021

CONTRIBUTORS

Charles A. Cefalu, MD
Harvard Medical School
Harvard Combined Orthopaedic Residency Program

Catherine Tsai, MD
University of California, San Diego Department of General Surgery

Stella J. Lee, MD
Harvard Medical School
Harvard Combined Orthopaedic Residency Program

Shaina A. Lipa, MD
Harvard Medical School
Harvard Combined Orthopaedic Residency Program

Max R. Haffner, MD
Department of Orthopaedic Surgery
University of California, Davis

Joseph B. Wick, MD
Department of Orthopaedic Surgery
University of California, Davis

George S. M. Dyer, MD
Associate Professor of Orthopaedic Surgery, Harvard Medical School
Attending Surgeon, Hand and Upper Extremity Service & Orthopaedic
Trauma Service, Brigham and Women's Hospital
Program Director, Harvard Combined Orthopaedic Residency Program

TABLE OF CONTENTS

DOMAIN 1: TRAUMA

1.1 BASICS

1.1.1 Damage control orthopaedics (DCO)

- Goals: minimize intraoperative hypotension & cerebral hypoperfusion (second hit phenomenon)
- DCO if ISS >40 w/o thoracic trauma, ISS <20 w/ thoracic trauma, GCS ≤8, multiple injuries w/ severe pelvic/abd trauma & hemorrhagic shock, b/l femur fx, pulmonary contusion noted on XR, hypothermia (<35°C), head injury w/ AIS ≥3, IL-6 > 500pg/dL
- Timing of definitive mgmt: pelvis/acetabular: 5-7d (no more than 3 weeks); ex-fix to IMN tibia: 7-10d; ex-fix to IMN femur: up to 3 weeks
- Transfusion ratio: 1:1:1 (pRBC : platelets : FFP)
  - Highest risk of viral transmission is hepatitis B (HBV)— 1:200,000
  - Donor blood is screened for: HIV-1 (1:1.9M), HIV-2, HBV, HCV (1:1.8M), West Nile virus, syphilis
- Normal: lactate <2.5 mmol/L, gastric mucosal pH >7.3, base deficit between -2 to +2
- Parameters for non-emergent OR: lactate <2.5mmol/L, HD stable off pressors, no hypoxemia/hypercapnia, normal INR, normothermia, normal UOP (>1mL/kg/hr)
- Injury severity score (ISS): $A^2 + B^2 + C^2$
  - A, B & C refer to top 3 most severely injured anatomic regions
  - DCO if ISS >40 w/o thoracic trauma OR >20 w/ thoracic trauma
- Risk factors for undertriage in trauma bay: female, age >65, 2+ comorbid conditions, nonwhite, GCS 15
- Risk factors for mortality after polytrauma in elderly patients: ISS, initial GCS ≤10, admission pH, admission lactate, *need for mechanical ventilation (#1)*
- After major trauma, women have poorer quality-of-life outcomes (e.g., higher PTSD, more sick leave time) than men
- Airbags protect against closed head injury (CHI), facial fx, flail chest, splenic rupture, but NOT pelvic fx

- 2-5d after injury: heightened inflammatory state, SIRS → CK release associated w/ DIC, MOSF & ARDS
- Children have *dampened systemic* physiologic inflammatory response but *robust local* inflammatory response
  - In children, multiorgan failure occurs early after admission, during resuscitation (thus, if urgent surgery needed do early after injury)
- Adults have *robust systemic* physiologic inflammatory response
  - In adults, multiorgan failure begins 48 hours after injury
    - Affects lungs first
- Early appropriate care (EAC): popularized in 2013
  - Identify & treat critical Ortho injuries (spine, femur, pelvis/tab fx w/in 36h) while minimizing 2nd hit, follow lab markers
  - Parameters: lactate <4, pH ≥7.25, base excess ≥ -5.5
  - Results: decreased delay to surgery, decreased complication rates, increased hospital revenues

1.1.2 Shock
- Neurogenic shock (disruption of sympathetic activity): hypotension & *bradycardia*
  - Tx: Dobutamine, Dopamine
- Spinal shock: temporary loss of spinal cord function below level of injury; in addition to loss of sympathetic tone (neurogenic shock), there is complete loss of sensorimotor function & reflexes (flaccid, areflexic paralysis)
  - Only when spinal shock has resolved (i.e., return of bulbocavernosus reflex) can you determine extent of spinal cord injury
- Adult avg blood volume: 5L; Peds: 75-80mL/kg
- Resuscitation: 2 large bore IVs, 2L crystalloid → no or transient response (type 3 or 4 shock) → Type (ABO, Rh) w/in 10min, crossmatched w/in 60 min
- Hemorrhagic shock: blood pressure differentiates Class II from III
  - Class II (15-30% blood volume loss/750-1500cc in avg adult): tachycardic (100-120 bpm), narrowed pulse pressure (vasoconstriction causes elevated DBP), *normotensive*, pH normal, UOP 20-30

- Tx: crystalloid
  - Class III (30-40% blood volume loss/1500-2000cc in avg adult): tachycardic (120-140 bpm), *hypotensive*, UOP 5-15, decreased pH, anxious/confused
    - Tx: crystalloid + blood products
- Lactate >2.5 signals end-organ hypoperfusion; <2.5 signals adequate resuscitation
- Septic shock vs hypovolemic shock: SVR increased in hypovolemic and decreased in septic

1.1.3 Open fracture

- Tetanus: give toxoid (0.5mL) regardless of age + 75U Ig if <5yo OR 125U Ig if 5-10yo OR 250U if >10yo
  - Give toxoid & Ig IM in separate locations
- No clinical advantage to OR <6h vs 6-24h
- 1-4% rate of MRSA colonization (low) for trauma patients at trauma centers
- Gustilo Anderson: true classification is best done after surgical debridement.
- Thorough debridement is best predictor of outcome
  - I: <1 cm; infection rate <1%
  - II: 1-10 cm
  - III: >10 cm, *segmental*, significant comminution, GSW, farm injury; infection rate 30%
    - IIIA: adequate soft tissue coverage
    - IIIB: free or regional soft tissue transfer (*flap*, not skin graft)
    - IIIC: vascular injury requiring *surgical repair*
- Antibiotics (w/in 6hrs)
  - I & II: 1st generation cephalosporin (gram positive coverage; e.g., cefazolin); x24h after closure
  - III: 1st generation cephalosporin & aminoglycoside (gram negative coverage; e.g., gentamicin); x72h after closure
  - Farm injury or bowel contamination: add penicillin (anaerobic coverage, Clostridia)
  - Water contamination: add Fluoroquinolone (e.g., Cipro)
- Flap coverage within *5 days* is desired (increased risk of infection if

3

delayed 7+ days)
- Irrigation: best with saline at low flow or pressure
  - No difference in infection or union rates w/ high pressure versus low pressure bulb irrigation
  - Saline w/ castile soap has decreased primary wound healing problems vs antibiotic irrigation solutions
- Bone defects from trauma (or infection)
  - Small: remove; if key articular piece → wash & replace
  - <3cm: non-vascularized gone graft
  - 5-12cm: vascularized bone graft (e.g., free fibula)
    - Slow rehab & high complication rate w/ free fibula
  - Shortening ok for humeral defects <4cm & femoral defects <8cm
    - Can then follow w/ distraction osteogenesis (done by intramembranous ossification)
      - Initiate distraction at *POD7* (allows for development of extraosseous blood supply & thus 2.6x mineralized callus volume—White & Kenwright) & distract at *1mm per day* (0.25mm QID in femur)
  - Masquelet technique: I&D, ORIF if trauma, PMMA antibiotic spacer to fill defect → staged bone grafting
    - Good for defects <25cm
    - Membrane around spacer forms at 6-8 weeks; harbors BMP-2: BMP-2 level peaks at *4 weeks* & returns to baseline at *6 months*
    - Optimal timing for removal of spacer & bone grafting at 4-6 weeks
    - PMMA antibiotic spacer: highest antibiotic concentration at *24 hours*, level remains bactericidal for up to *4 months*
      - Vancomycin is time-dependent; tobramycin is concentration-dependent
      - Maximum recommended concentration (to avoid systemic toxicity): 10.5 grams of vancomycin or 12.5 grams of tobramycin per 40mg of PMMA

4

1.1.4 Gunshot wound

- Fracture secondary to low-velocity GSW (<2,000 feet per second): local wound care, oral antibiotic, standard management of fracture as if it was a closed injury
  - For example: humeral shaft GSW fracture with radial nerve palsy: antibiotic, coaptation splint, observation
- Intraarticular GSW: I&D, retrieval of bullet fragments to prevent plumbism
- GSW to hip is most commonly associated with bowel perforation → laparotomy
- GSW to spine: antibiotic for 24-48 hours (longer if there is intestinal injury—1 week)
  - Decompression fusion only if (1) progressive neurologic deficit and/or (2) instability
- GSW w/ vascular injury needs bony stability
  - GSW w/ vascular injury portends increased risk of infection
- Associated acetabular fx type & bowel injury are both independent predictors of infection in setting of GSW
- During initial exploration of GSW, if nerve is transected → surgical treatment at *1 to 3 weeks* post injury
  - If not transected, obs for recovery x 2-3 months
- Ulnar nerve injury from GSW has worst functional recovery after repair

1.1.5 Lower extremity amputation

- LEAP:
  - IMN is better than ex-fix
  - Sickness Impact Profile (SIP) & return to work not significantly different between amp & limb salvage at 2y
  - Mangled foot/ankle injuries requiring free tissue transfer have lower SIP than BKA
  - Strongest determinant of satisfaction following amp is ability to return to work
    - METALS study (military population): higher rates of return to vigorous activity in amputation group
  - Severity of soft tissue injury is strongest determinant of amputation.

- o Scoring systems not great; plantar sensation is NOT an absolute indication for amp; social/family/socioeconomic factors most predictive of long-term outcome
- o No differences between amputation & limb reconstruction (i.e., return to work, functional outcomes, cost)
- o After severe lower extremity injury, *psychosocial* function does not improve with time
- o Hyperbaric oxygen therapy for soft tissue injury / defect: contraindication includes insulin pump, pacemaker & ICD
- o Absolute indications for amp: 1) blunt or contaminated traumatic amp, 2) mangled extremity in critically ill patient in shock, 3) crushed extremity w/ arterial injury & warm ischemia >6 hours
- o Relative indications for amp: 1) severe soft tissue or bone loss, 2) transection of major motor nerves, 3) open tibia fx w/ serious associated polytrauma, 4) ipsilateral foot injury with prolonged course to get soft tissue coverage
- The more proximal the amputation, the greater the energy expenditure required for ambulation
  - o *Unilateral* transfemoral amputation (AKA) results in higher energy expenditure for ambulation (65%) compared to *bilateral* transtibial amputations (BKAs) (40%)
    - ▪ Vascular transfemoral (100%)
    - ▪ Through knee is worse than AKA, slower walking speeds than BKA
  - o Syme (ankle disarticulation) is the most energy-efficient (15%)
    - ▪ Used to treat forefoot gangrene in diabetics
  - o Traumatic BKA (avg transtibial, 25%) vs vascular BKA (40%)
  - o Traumatic: short transtibial (40%), long transtibial (10%)
- Better wound healing if albumin >3, ABI >0.45, lymphocyte count >1,500, toe pressure >40, transcutaneous oxygen tension >30
- AKA: adductor myodesis to femur improves outcomes & prosthetic fitting
- BKA: bridging synostosis (Ertl) transtibial amputation provides equivalent functional outcomes but higher complications compared to traditional non-bone-bridging amputation (modified Burgess)
  - o Thought that bridge would increase end-bearing capacity w/ osteomyoplasty

6

- o Leave "dog ears" alone: blood supply to flap
- In children, *knee disarticulation* is most proximal level at which walking speed can be maintained without significantly increasing energy expenditure
- Syme amputation: any amputation distal to BKA requires patent PT artery for wound healing
  - o Requires stable & viable heel pad (most important)
- Chopart amputation (through transverse tarsal joints)
  - o Equinus deformity: Achilles tendon lengthening (most important) & transfer tibialis anterior to talar neck
- Lisfranc amputation (through TMT joints)
  - o Equinovarus deformity: maintain insertion of peroneus brevis
- Phantom limb pain: mirror therapy
- Fibular abduction: common complication w/ tibial myodesis techniques, thought to represent syndesmotic instability
- NPWT: most effective at 125mmHg
  - o Decreases open tib infection rate, increases perfusion after fasciotomy, accelerates granulation tissue formation, faster STSG incorporation, helps "at risk" wounds (decreased likelihood of secondary complex soft tissue recon)
  - o But DOES NOT extend soft tissue coverage window
- In kids, bone overgrowth is MCC; prevent by performing disarticulation or using epiphyseal cap to cover medullary canal
- Postamputation neuroma pain: targeted muscle reinnervation (TMR)

1.2 UPPER EXTREMITY TRAUMA

1.2.1 Scapula fracture
- Associated w/ increased ISS, rib fx (52%)
- Non-op: sling x 2 wks f/b early ROM/PT
- Operative indications: glenohumeral instability (>25% glenoid involvement w/ HH subluxation OR >5mm glenoid articular step-off, displaced scapula neck fx, open fx, loss of RTC function, coracoid fx w/ >1cm displacement, "double disruption" of superior shoulder suspensory complex, glenopolar angle <22°)
- Operative approach: Judet most common—plane between Is

(suprascapular n) and Tm (axillary n)
- Scapulothoracic dissociation: outcome is dependent on neurologic injury; most often associated w/ mortality (10%)
    - If return of neuro function is unlikely, early amp is recommended

1.2.2 Clavicle fracture
- Clavicle is 1st to ossify, medial clavicle fuses last (age 25yo)
- Scapula ER prevents GT impingement on acromion
- Sling, not figure-of-8
- Predictors of nonunion: female, displacement, comminution, advanced age, shortening >2cm
    - Displacement (>100%) is biggest RF for nonunion
    - Relative indications for OR: >2cm shortening, b/l displaced fx, BPI, closed head injury, seizure disorder, polytrauma
- Nonoperative: higher symptomatic malunion & nonunion (10-15% NU rate w/ non-op), lower functional outcomes (Constant & DASH scores); Operative with higher TTU, Constant & DASH scores at all time points, lower NU rate (1-5%); however, initial operative Tx associated w/ increased healthcare costs.
    - Risk of infection ~4.8% w/ operative
        - Risk factors: illicit drug use, DM, prior shoulder surgery
    - Malunion defined as >3cm shortening, >1cm translation, >30° angulation
    - Operative TTU ~16wks, Non-op TTU ~28 wks
- Decreased shoulder *strength* & *endurance* if midshaft heals with >2cm shortening. *Equal ROM* between non-op and operative
- Acromioclavicular (AC) joint: superior & posterior AC ligaments provide anteroposterior stability; coracoclavicular (CC) ligaments (conoid—4.5cm from ACJ—is medial to trapezoid—3cm from ACJ) provide superoinferior stability
    - Conoid is stronger than trapezoid
    - Clavicle rotates 40-50° posteriorly w/ shoulder elevation; 8° is through AC joint, rest through scapulothoracic & SC joint
    - Injury to PS AC ligament: predominantly posterior instability of clavicle

- Congenital pseudarthrosis of clavicle: usually middle-third of *right* clavicle
- Sternoclavicular dislocation
  - Posterior ligaments resistant to A-P displacement; Anterior ligaments resistant to superior displacement
    - Medial clavicle excision: keep ≤15mm so as not to hit costoclavicular ligament (stabilizes medial clavicle)
  - Generally nonoperative except for posterior SC dislocation with compression of trachea (dyspnea) & esophagus (dysphagia): closed vs open reduction with thoracic surgery available

1.2.3 Proximal humerus fracture

- Humeral neck-shaft angle 130°, retroversion 30°. Glenoid w/ average retroversion 5° (range 10ant-27retro), upward tilt of 5°
- "1 part" displacement: 5mm or 45°
  - Non-op shows return to baseline ASES & functional status at 1 year, but ROM diminished compared to contralateral (ER/IR decreased, FF preserved)
- Isolated GT/LT fx: think ant/posterior dislocation
  - Axillary and/or musculocutaneous neuropraxia common (axillary nerve 5-7cm from acromion)
    - Usually transient—obs x 6-8 weeks, then EMG if no improvement
- Posteromedial calcar pike (metaphyseal extension) >8mm is predictor of intact vascular supply
  - Posterior humeral circumflex artery (*PHCA*) is predominant blood supply to humeral head (64%)
  - In order of predictive accuracy of HH ischemia (Hertel criteria): calcar length <8mm, disrupted medial hinge, HH angulation >45°, head-split
    - Note, does NOT necessarily predict development of AVN
- Young: CRPP/ORIF if able, otherwise hemiarthroplasty (if no glenohumeral arthritis) or TSA (if glenohumeral arthritis).
  - Hemiarthroplasty is especially indicated for head-splitting fx
  - ORIF: screw cut-out & intraarticular penetration is most common complication

- Adding an inferomedial screw to purchase calcar is key to preventing varus collapse of fracture
- Elderly or history of rotator cuff tear / arthropathy or elderly w/ initial varus angulation >60°: rTSA
  - Increasing age is risk factor for poor outcome at 1 year
  - GT repair/healing is shown to improve *ER and FF* following rTSA
  - Superior edge of pectoralis major insertion (PMI) guides humeral prosthesis height & retroversion
    - Normal: 30° retroversion, 130-140° neck-shaft angle
    - PMI is 5.6cm distal to superior aspect of humeral head
  - Avoid ER of shoulder after surgery to protect subscapularis repair (stretch repair)
    - Also avoid activation of subscapularis (e.g., pushing oneself up from chair)
    - rTSA dislocation (usually anterior) is associated with subscapularis rupture / insufficiency postoperative (dislocation with arm in extension, ADD & ER)
      - US can help detect postoperative subscapularis rupture
- Outcomes of ORIF or shoulder replacement depend on healing of greater tuberosity: poor outcomes if malunion or nonunion
  - Medial edge of GT is 10mm lateral to humeral canal axis
  - Incorrect placement results in abnormal ER kinematics & 8-fold increase in torque requirements
  - Passive ER puts most stress on LT
- Isolated greater tuberosity fracture: ORIF if >5mm displacement; rotator cuff pulls GT superior (block abduction) & posterior (block ER)
- Deltoid splitting approach with increased rate of axillary n injury versus deltopec
- Malunion: usually varus & apex-anterior; poor outcomes if you do TSA w/ varus malunited fx, do rTSA instead
- Nonunion: most common w/ 2-part fx; if good bone stock, revision ORIF; if poor bone stock → arthroplasty

1.2.4 Humeral shaft fracture
- Holstein-Lewis: spiral fracture of distal one-third humeral shaft →

high incidence of radial nerve neuropraxia (22%)
- Closed treatment with functional bracing: fracture site mobility at 6 weeks is associated with nonunion (>90% go to nonunion)
  - Non-op parameters: <20°apex anterior, varus/valgus <30°, shortening <3cm
- Heavier patients w/ increased risk of varus collapse because increased bending moment
- Iatrogenic radial nerve injury during ORIF is associated with surgical approach used (NOT time to fixation)
  - Anterolateral—lowest risk f/b posterior f/b lateral (highest risk)
- ORIF with plate (4.5mm): open fracture, vascular injury requiring repair, brachial plexus injury (higher nonunion if nonoperative), floating elbow, bilateral humeral shaft fractures, polytrauma (allows early weight bearing), compartment syndrome, periprosthetic fx at tip of stem
  - Full crutch weightbearing (w/ polytrauma) shown to have no effect on union
  - Anterior approach: proximal- & middle-third humeral shaft
  - Posterior approach: middle- & distal-third humeral shaft, radial nerve lies *medial* to long & lateral heads of triceps & *proximal* to deep head of triceps
    - Follow posterior antebrachial cutaneous nerve (PABCN) proximally to find radial nerve
  - Cable or wire fixation: fixation proximal to inferior edge of latissimus dorsi reduces risk of iatrogenic radial nerve injury
- IMN: pathologic fracture
  - Higher total complications (i.e., shoulder stiffness, shoulder impingement, & reoperation rate compared to plate)
    - No difference in nerve injury or ASES functional scores between IMN & ORIF
  - Lateral to medial distal interlock: radial nerve
    - Radial nerve crosses posterior humerus from 14-21cm from top of HH, safe zone above & below; crosses posterior to humerus 20cm above medial epicondyle & crosses lateral IMS 14cm above lateral epicondyle & 10cm proximal to RC joint
  - Anterior to posterior distal interlock: musculocutaneous nerve
  - Nonunion after non-op or surgery: revision ORIF (compression

plating) w/ bone grafting (gold standard)
- For very proximal/distal NU, can do dual plating (92-100% union at 16 weeks)
- For recalcitrant NU or severe osteopenia or bone loss, can try fibula allo/autograft

- Radial nerve palsy
  - Closed humeral shaft: likely radial nerve neuropraxia → Observation
    - 90% resolve by 3 months; if not → EMG
    - Surgical exploration if not improved over 4-6 months
  - Open humeral shaft: likely radial nerve neurotmesis → exploration & repair
  - Brachioradialis is first muscle to recover (wrist extension in radial deviation), followed by ECRL; extensor indicis proprius (EIP) is last (index finger MCP hyperextension).
  - Non-op NU rate: 2-33%, Operative NU rate 5-10%
    - *Vitamin D deficiency* is major metabolic risk factor for NU

1.2.5 Distal humerus fracture
- Obtain traction radiographs or CT to better assess fracture pattern
- Young patient with good bone stock: ORIF
- Elderly patient with comminuted, osteoporotic bone and/or comminuted bicolumnar fx: total elbow arthroplasty (TEA)
  - *Lower reoperation rate* when compared to ORIF, better ROM vs ORIF, better Mayo Elbow & DASH scores than ORIF, shorter surgical time w/ TEA vs ORIF
  - When deciding between ORIF vs TEA, avoid olecranon osteotomy during exposure as this may affect TEA; instead, use triceps sparing or split approach
  - If concomitant olecranon fx with distal humerus fx, ok to excise instead of repair (outcomes are equal to excision w/ TEA vs ORIF w/ TEA)
- Chevron osteotomy: 2cm apex-distal to triceps insertion/olecranon tip in bare area of ulna.
  - Angle screw slightly medially to account for varus angulation of proximal ulna.

- o Most common complication is *symptomatic hardware*
- o AIN is at risk with olecranon osteotomy
- Postoperative ulnar neuropathy is associated with intraoperative ulnar nerve transposition.
  - o Only do if symptomatic preoperatively
- ORIF: no ROH before 18 months; most common complication is stiffness—usually get 75% back, 30-130° needed for ADLs
  - o For improved flexion, can release posterior band of MCL & posterior capsule + osteophyte excision
  - o Literature now supports *parallel* plating w/ all distal screws through plate
  - o 25% rate of 'unsatisfactory' outcomes
- Lateral condyle fx (non-op): immobilize in supination; medial condyle fx (non-op): immobilize in pronation

1.2.6 Capitellar fracture
- Coronal shear fracture of capitellum with extension into trochlea (double arc sign): requires exposure of entire lateral column, elevating off common extensors & capsule
  - o Most common complication: stiffness (flexion contracture)
  - o Disruption of posterior perforating vessels → AVN of capitellum
  - o Disruption of LUCL → valgus posterolateral rotatory instability

1.2.7 Elbow dislocation
- Mechanism same as terrible triad: fall onto outstretched arm (axial compression, forearm supination & valgus load)
  - o After closed reduction, splint in *elbow flexion & pronation* to prevent subluxation.
  - o For *simple* dx, can treat closed w/ splinting in 90° flexion for 5-10d f/b early therapy
    - ▪ Recurrent instability rate low (1-2%)
- Usually posterolateral dislocation: structures fail from lateral to medial
  - o LCL fails by ligament avulsion off lateral epicondyle
- Most common complication for simple and complex patterns is *loss of terminal extension*

- Rehab (non-op or ORIF): supervised active & active-assist motion through stable ROM arc, extension block brace x 3-4 wks, light duty use at 2 wks
- Pediatric: most common associated fracture is medial epicondyle fracture
  o >5mm displacement (relative indication) or incarcerated medial epicondyle (absolute indication): ORIF
    ▪ Ulnar nerve is at risk of entrapment
  o Pediatric simple elbow dislocation after successful closed reduction: splint for 10 days, followed by protected ROM
- Anatomic note: MCL is primary restraint to valgus at 30-120°; anterior MCL attaches 18mm distal to tip of coronoid; LCL insertion lateral epicondyle to supinator crest

1.2.8 Terrible triad
- Mechanism: fall onto outstretched hand with forearm in *supination* & *valgus* thrust
- In general, address radial head first, followed by coronoid, then LCL, and finally MCL
  o Fix radial head if <3 fragments; replace radial head if ≥3 fragments; never perform acute resection
  o Coronoid fracture: if fracture is ≤50% of height, may not have to repair (2016 OITE)
    ▪ Coronoid avulsion that is <10% of entire coronoid does not require repair
  o Always repair / reconstruct LCL; repair MCL last if there is persistent valgus instability
- If only LCL is repaired, splint in flexion / pronation; if both LCL & MCL are repaired, splint in flexion / neutral
- Better outcomes if active elbow ROM beginning 48 hrs postop; full flexion ok, but limit extension to 30°

1.2.9 Coronoid fracture
- Anterior bundle of MUCL inserts on sublime tubercle (anteromedial facet of coronoid)
  o Fracture of anteromedial facet and/or injury to anterior bundle → varus instability, varus posteromedial rotatory instability

14

(LCL usually also torn)
- Immobilization & early ROM if stable elbow joint
- ORIF if unstable elbow joint

1.2.10 Olecranon fracture
- Tension band
  - Only for simple transverse patterns (if comminution or complex—e.g., Monteggia—needs plate/screw construct)
  - Most common complication is symptomatic implants (40-80%)
  - Penetration of K-wire through anterior (trans) cortex of ulna → AIN injury & mechanical block to pronosupination
    - Obs x 6 months or can explore if suspect injury or obvious hardware prominence
- Elderly patient with comminuted, osteoporotic bone: excision with triceps advancement (if fracture involves <30-50% of articular surface)
  - Can also treat non-op with cast
- Heterotopic ossification associated with elbow fractures is higher in patients with closed head injury
  - HO prophylaxis
    - Indomethacin
    - Single radiation (700cGy dose): either 4 hours before or within 72 hours after surgery
- Olecranon fx after low-energy fall in kids: think osteogenesis imperfecta

1.2.11 Monteggia fracture
- Apex of ulna fracture is generally in same direction as radial head dislocation
  - Bado 2 (posterior) associated w/ highest complication rate & worst prognosis
- Annular ligament interposition in radiocapitellar joint may block anatomic reduction
- PIN is at greatest risk after Monteggia fracture: radial deviation of hand with wrist extension (from pull of mobile wad; BR and ECRL w/ innervation from radial nerve proper)
- Isolated ulna shaft fx: non-op if <50% translation, <10° angulation

1.2.12 Radial head fracture
- Fracture with no or minimal (<2mm) displacement: early ROM
- <25-30% joint surface can also excise if symptomatic
- Fracture with >2mm displacement
  - Not comminuted (<3 fragments): ORIF
    - Safe (nonarticular) zone for hardware placement: 90° arc from radial styloid to Lister's tubercle.
      - Regardless of approach, keep forearm in *neutral* rotation for plate application in bare area
    - Kocher approach: anconeus(radial n)/ECU(PIN). Less risk of PIN injury than Kaplan because more posterior but more risk of LUCL violation
    - Kaplan approach: ECRB(radial n)/EDC(PIN). Better visualization of coronoid than Kocher
  - Comminuted (≥3 fragments): radial head replacement
  - No acute radial head resection → proximal radial migration resulting in distal ulnar impaction syndrome (especially if there is associated DRUJ injury)
- Essex-Lopresti: radial head fracture with DRUJ dislocation & disruption of interosseous membrane
- Lateral approaches to elbow: pronate forearm to pull PIN nerve anteriorly away from field
- Post-traumatic elbow stiffness: supervised therapy w/ static or dynamic progressive splinting over 6-month period has greatest improvement on DASH and functional ROM

1.2.13 Adult both bone forearm fracture (BBFF)
- Isolated ulna fx: non-op if <50% displacement & <10° angulation—equivalent to operative
- Objective of ORIF is to restore radial bow
- Central band is most important ligament of interosseous membrane (IOM)
- Best plate to use is 3.5mm LC-DCP
  - 4.5mm plate has higher risk of refracture
  - Do not remove hardware before 15 months; after plate removal, consider bracing to prevent refracture

- Single incision has higher risk of synostosis; decreased risk w/ 2-incision
  - o Resection of heterotopic ossification can be performed as early as 6 months postoperative
  - o Mature HO is characterized by sharp cortical margins on xrays
- Only use bone graft if there is *segmental* bone loss of radius; large segmental defect: vascularized fib graft—lower rate of infection than non-vascularized allograft strut
- Bridge plate osteosynthesis: construct is flexible & axially stable
  - o Don't use IMN—difficulty restoring radial bow & thus loss of forearm rotation
- Ok to fix & close primarily for GA type 1-3 fx if able
- NWB x 6 weeks

1.2.14 Distal radius fracture (DRF)
- Formal PT after injury or surgery does not change outcomes
- High energy fx associated w/ acute CTS in 30% (paresthesias, inability to oppose thumb); low energy in 1-2%
- McQueen parameters: age, initial displacement, dorsal comminution, ulnar variance
- Normal: volar tilt 11°, radial height 13mm, radial inclination 23°
- New AAOS/ASSH CPGs (Moderate recs): Operative if <65yo & post-reduction w/ shortening >3mm, dorsal tilt >10°, gap >2mm
- Non-op if <5mm Radial shortening, <5° dorsal tilt or within 20° of contralateral
- CRPS prevention: vitamin C 500mg QD for 50 days
  - o CRPS type I: no identifiable nerve lesions
  - o CRPS type II (causalgia): identifiable nerve lesions
- EPL rupture: inability to lift thumb *off* table with palm flat
  - o Spontaneous rupture is most often associated with nonoperative treatment of nondisplaced DRF in cast
  - o Treatment: transfer EIP to EPL
- Volar plate fixation is preferred
  - o EPL rupture: screw penetration through dorsal cortex
  - o FPL rupture: plate placement distal to watershed line & protrusion of plate beyond volar lip of distal radius; 2nd most

common rupture after FPL is IF FDP
- ▪ Tx: FDS to FPL transfer
- Dorsal plate fixation reserved for intraarticular DRF with significant dorsal comminution

1.2.15 Distal radioulnar joint (DRUJ) injury

- DRUJ dx (direction describes ulna): dorsal > volar
- Ulna goes dorsal w/in notch during pronation (volar RUL tight), volar w/in notch during supination (dorsal RUL tight)
- Galeazzi fracture: ECU interposition may prevent reduction of DRUJ
  - o Radial shaft fracture <7.5cm from articular surface has higher incidence of DRUJ instability
  - o DRUJ is most stable in supination
- DRF + ulnar styloid fracture + DRUJ instability: fix DRF first, then assess DRUJ
  - o If DRUJ is stable, immobilize in supination (if DRUJ dislocates dorsally) or pronation (if DRUJ dislocates volarly)
  - o If DRUJ in unstable, CRPP or ORIF of DRUJ
    - ▪ If still non-anatomic, then CRPP or ORIF of ulnar styloid fracture
- TFCC has 7 components: *volar & dorsal radioulnar ligaments* (primary stabilizers of DRUJ), central articular disc, meniscal homologue, ulnolunate & ulnotriquetral ligaments, ulnar collateral ligament, ECU tendon sheath
  - o Like knee meniscus, peripheral TFCC is vascular (→ repair) while central TFCC is avascular (→ debridement)
  - o TFCC tear: positive ulnar fovea sign

1.3 LOWER EXTREMITY TRAUMA

1.3.1 Hip dislocation

- Normal: femoral H-N angle 130 +/- 7°, version 10 +/- 7°
- High energy deceleration mechanism w/ posterior dx associated w/ thoracic aortic injury in 8%
- Posterior dislocation: clinically, hip is in flexion, ADD & IR
- Anterior dislocation: hip is in flexion, ABD & ER
- CT after reduction to evaluate for impaction, fractures or loose bodies

- If open reduction is required, approach from direction of dislocation since soft tissues / capsule are already compromised
- Posterior approach: femoral head blood supply (lateral epiphyseal vessels) are within 15mm of insertion of short external rotators
- If simple dx, treat w/ PWB x 4-6 weeks
- Goal reduction *<6hrs*
- Complications
  - 20% risk of post-traumatic arthritis w/ simple dx; higher if complex
  - ONFH: 5-40% incidence; increased risk with increased time to reduction
  - Sciatic injury: 8-20% incidence; increased risk w/ increased time to reduction
  - Recurrent dx: <2%

1.3.2 Femoral neck fracture (FNF)
- Young: closed or open reduction internal fixation
  - Most common complication: osteonecrosis (main blood supply is MFCA)
    - Secondary blood supply is IGA
    - Risk factor for osteonecrosis: preoperative degree of displacement
  - Most common malreduction: varus
  - CRPP: inverted triangle with inferior screw in posteroinferior neck adjacent to calcar just above level of LT to avoid stress riser
  - FAITH trial: SHS w/ higher *AVN* than cannulated screws (9% vs 6%) & increased LOS vs CRPP, but equivalent union
    - Smokers and basicervical do benefit from SHS—lower rate of reoperation than cannulated screws
  - Posterior "in-out-in" screw: doesn't matter (no adverse effect)
- FNF in elderly, sedentary: hemiarthroplasty
  - Preoperative fascia iliaca block decreases overall narcotic use, delirium & length of hospital stay
  - Non-displaced FNF: T1 MRI is best but if pacemaker → bone scan 72h after injury
  - Preop mobility is best predictor of post-op mortality

19

- Chronic renal failure → ~50% mortality at 2y
- Factors influencing ability to both ambulate & live independently at 1yr post-op: age 50-80, ASA 1 rating, not requiring walking aid prior to fx, non-smoker or former smoker, acceptable implant placement, not requiring revision
- FNF in elderly, active: total hip arthroplasty (THA)
  - THA vs hemiarthroplasty: higher dislocation but lower reoperation rates with THA; better functional outcomes with THA
- Femoral neck nonunion in young: valgus intertrochanteric osteotomy, which converts vertical fracture line (shear force) to horizontal fracture line (compressive force)
- Femoral neck nonunion in elderly: THA
- Femoral neck stress fracture
  - Compression-side: protected weight bearing
    - Consider CRPP if >50% femoral neck is involved
  - Tension-side: closed reduction percutaneous pinning (CRPP)

1.3.3 Peritrochanteric hip fracture
- Displacement: proximal fragment is flexed (iliopsoas), abducted (gluteus medius & minimus) & externally rotated (short external rotators)
- 1st year mortality 30%, 6% while inpatient
  - Increased if >85yo, >2d before surgery, medical comorbidities
  - Surgery <24hrs decreases *both* 30-day and 1-year mortality
- DHS: tip-apex distance >25mm is predictor for failure of fixation (if >40mm 60% rate of hardware failure)
  - Do for simple IT fx (31-A1), otherwise CMN is optimal choice
    - Also better mobility at 1 year vs SHS
  - 2-hole equivalent to 4-hole DHS
  - No DHS for reverse obliquity intertrochanteric hip fracture
  - No SHS if lateral wall < 20.5mm
    - 21% incidence of lateral wall fx & 22% incidence of reoperation if SHS used
  - L-sided fx needs derotation screw to prevent apex-anterior malreduction secondary to torque as SHS s placed

- Increased use of CMN over DHS for intertrochanteric hip fractures because of higher Medicare reimbursement
- Stable intertrochanteric hip fracture: DHS or short locked cephalomedullary nail (CMN)
- Long CMN for unstable fractures: reverse obliquity, subtrochanteric extension, comminuted lateral femoral wall
  - Supine: easier to obtain fluoroscopic images & assess rotation; better in polytrauma (protect spine, access to other injuries)
  - Lateral: easier to identify entry point; facilitate fracture reduction
- Helical blade vs screw: blade with higher rates of medial migration/superolateral cutout vs screw
- For CMN of proximal femur fractures, a posterior starting point increases risk of impingement & penetration of anterior cortex of distal femur
  - Anterior perforation of distal femur can also occur when there is a large mismatch between radius of curvature of nail & femoral shaft.
  - Taller patients usually w/ less of a bow (increased ROC) & matches nail
- Most common deformity / malunion with CMN of peritrochanteric fractures is varus & flexion (procurvatum)
- No differences between short vs long CMN other than cost (higher with long CMN)
- For isolated fracture of greater trochanter, MRI is better than CT at identifying intertrochanteric extension
- Bisphosphonates: lateral cortical thickening of subtrochanteric region.
- Subtroch fx-nonunion: ORIF w/ DCS or 95° blade plate & bone grafting (allows correction of varus deformity)
  - If use CMN: increased r/o iatrogenic fx & nonunion; but plate w/ risk of hardware failure
- *Delay to surgery* (>2 midnights) & *delirium* most significantly affect length of stay
  - *ASA* classification, NOT Charlson comorbidity index shown to predict LOS

1.3.4 Femoral shaft fracture

- As high as *10% (6-9%)* of patients have ipsilateral FNF; can be initially missed up to 50% of time
  - Fx are often *vertical, basicervical, non-displaced*
    - ID w/ 2mm fine-cut CT or IR/ER views on fluoro
- Treat FNF first, followed by femoral shaft
- Each femoral shaft fracture can lose 1250cc EBL
- Fat embolism syndrome: petechiae, hypoxemia & altered mental status
- After antegrade IMN of femoral shaft fracture, *quadriceps & abductors* are weakest muscle groups.
- Piriformis entry nail: if entry point is too anterior (*6mm*), there is increased risk of iatrogenic fracture.
  - However, cheating anterior will improve trajectory of cephalomedullary screw
  - Using a piriformis entry (straight) nail for a trochanteric starting point can lead to varus malalignment
- Most common complication after IMN is malrotation (malunion)
  - CT is best at diagnosing malrotation, defined as >15° rotational malalignment compared to contralateral extremity
  - Fracture table increases risk for *internal* malrotation.
  - Comminution also a RF for malrotation.
  - After IMN:
    - If lower extremity IR is increased: either too much femoral anteversion of proximal fragment (think anteversion ~ IR) or too much IR of distal fragment
    - If lower extremity ER is increased: either too much femoral retroversion of proximal fragment (think retroversion ~ ER) or too much ER of distal fragment
- Femoral shaft nonunion: compression plating +/- bone grafting
- Shortening femur deviates mechanical axis medially; lengthening femur deviates mechanical axis laterally.
- Good indication for BMP in fracture surgery: geriatric supracondylar femur fx.
- Complications:
  - Antegrade (hip pain) vs retrograde (knee pain, locking screw irritation)
  - Most common complication after IMN in peds: peroneal palsy

(associated w/ *longer OR time* and *heavier weight*).
- o   RF for nonunion: NSAIDs, smoking
    - ▪   Nonunion treatment: reamed exchange nailing OR plate augmentation

1.3.5 Distal femur fracture
- Distal femur is in 7° valgus
- If fracture is intraarticular, obtain CT to evaluate for coronal fracture of femoral condyle (Hoffa fracture)
    - o   Hoffa: lateral condyle more frequently involved than medial condyle, but medial condyle is more often open
- Golf club / hockey stick deformity: if locking plate is placed too posterior distally, it will cause distal fracture fragment to translate medially as locking screws are inserted

1.3.6 Patella fracture
- Blood supply: *geniculate* arteries arising primarily from popliteal artery (inferior to superior flow)
- Tension band fixation: bending K-wires both proximally & distally will minimize wire migration.
- Strongest construct is cannulated screw with tension band wiring; weakest is isolated cerclage wiring
- Partial patellectomy: severely comminuted inferior or superior *pole* fracture when ORIF is not possible.
    - o   If performed, CR TKA is contraindicated
- Predictors of fixation failure: increasing age, fixation with K-wires (compared to screws)
- Bipartite patella: most commonly *superolateral*; smooth cortical borders; fibrocartilage between 2 fragments
- Pediatric patella sleeve fracture
    - o   ORIF, usually with suture fixation
- Most common complications: 1) anterior knee pain 2) symptomatic hardware (20% need ROH)

1.3.7 Knee dislocation
- Common peroneal nerve & popliteal artery are at risk

- o CPN injury associated w/ *lateral dx*; PCL and LCL injury associated w/ *medial dx*
- o Anterior (most common): usually results in intimal injury; posterior (2nd most common) often results in arterial transection
- o SPN: peroneal brevis & longus; sensation over dorsum of foot except 1st dorsal web space
- o DPN: TA, EHL, EDL, peroneus tertius; sensation over 1st dorsal web space
- Acute treatment of associated ligamentous injuries is associated w/ higher rate of *anterior knee instability* and *flexion deficits*
  - o No difference (acute vs delayed treatment) w/ regard to nerve injury, need for lysis of adhesions / manipulation under anesthesia
- After closed reduction, if palpable pulses (even if faint) with adequate perfusion → ABI
  - o ABI <0.9: advanced imaging such as CTA; vascular consult if evidence of arterial injury
- After closed reduction, if pulseless with poor perfusion → vascular consult & surgical exploration, not advanced imaging
- Posterolateral dislocation: buttonholing of medial femoral condyle through capsule (i.e., dimple sign) can prevent closed reduction → open reduction
- Multiligamentous knee injury: early arthroscopy increases risk for compartment syndrome
  - o Capsular defects → fluid extravasation into thigh or lower leg compartments
  - o Morbid obesity is a poor prognostic factor
- Traumatic knee arthrotomy
  - o 175mL saline load test: detect 99% of cases
  - o 155mL: detect 95% of cases

1.3.8 Tibial plateau fracture
- o Lateral plateau is convex & proximal; medial plateau is concave & distal (and larger A→P width)
  - o Lateral plateau fracture: lateral meniscal tear is associated with >10mm articular depression

- o Vascular and CPN injuries are most common with Schatzker IV (medial plateau fracture): medial fragment remains attached to femur (knee dx equivalent → do ABIs)
- o Associated meniscal injury: partial meniscectomy for radial tear, meniscal repair for longitudinal tear
- o Primary goal is to restore joint stability / maintain limb mechanical axis; anatomic articular reduction is secondary goal.
  - o Primary determinant of surgical outcome (and limiting development of degenerative changes) is maintenance of mechanical axis (need < 5° malalignment)
- o After leg fasciotomy, timing to definitive ORIF does not influence infection risk
- o Calcium phosphate: less subsidence than even autograft and PMMA.
- o Calcium sulfate: not preferred because of fast resorption & serous wound drainage
- o Risk factors for infection after ORIF: male, smoker, high ASA, pulmonary disease, bicondylar pattern
- o Hybrid external fixator: higher malunion rates (51%) compared to bicolumnar plating, higher superficial infection rate
  - o Bicondylar plating: higher deep infection rate than hybrid ex-fix
  - o Both w/ similar ROM & functional outcomes
- o Good outcomes w/ non-op if condylar widening <5mm, <2mm articular incongruity, <5° varus/valgus laxity
- o Tibia plateau fx in setting of osteoporosis & existing DJD: if questionable ability to maintain weightbearing precautions (i.e., lives alone), TKA w/ augments +/- stem is an option for immediate weightbearing
- o TKR after tibial plateau fracture: higher complications, equivalent patient-reported outcomes & satisfaction (vs primary TKR).

1.3.9 Tibial shaft fracture

- • IMN starting point: AP view (just medial to lateral tibial eminence) & lateral view (reflection point between tibial plateau & anterior tibial metaphysis)
- • Proximal-third: *valgus & procurvatum* deformity (EM pulls proximal fragment into extension, pes pulls distal fragment into flexion & valgus)
  - o 60% rate of malunion
  - o Place blocking (Poller) screws *posterior* (to prevent

procurvatum) & *lateral* (to prevent valgus) in proximal
fragment.
- Always place blocking screws at *concave side of resultant deformity*
- Another way to think of this is to place line down shaft & another in the plane of the fx, then place blocking screws in the acute angle of the metaphyseal segment
  o Suprapatellar/semiextended nailing (procurvatum), lateral entry point (valgus), unicortical plating (both), universal distractor (both).
- Suprapatellar relaxes the EM
  o No difference between suprapatellar & infrapatellar with respect to knee pain, but improved *coronal translation & angulation w/ suprapatellar*
  o No difference in knee pain with patellar split vs paratendinous; unpredictable relief of knee pain with nail removal
  o IMN starting point (also applicable to femur anterograde IMN): lateral: susceptible to varus malalignment; medial: susceptible to valgus malalignment
  o Theory that reaming disrupts endosteal blood flow & thus should not do in open fx, but no effect on nonunion, reoperation rate, or infection
  o SPRINT: no association of thermal necrosis w/ reaming under tourniquet (maybe prevention of microemboli)
- Reamed nailing w/ decreased need for future bone grafting or exchange nailing vs unreamed (in closed fx)
  o Risk factors for nonunion requiring reoperation: *transverse fx, open fx, <50% cortical contact* (gapping), *stainless steel nail* (not really used much anymore)
- No healing at 9 months: dynamize; if not axially stable→exchange reamed nailing w/ BMP7
  o Disruption of proximal tib-fib joint w/ shaft fx is a poor prognostic factor
- 63% incidence of open fx, 36% CPN injury (70% of which don't recover from time of injury), 29% compartment syndrome
- Distal-third:
  o Plating of distal tibia is best method to prevent malalignment

- o Second best method is IMN of tibia & plating of fibula
  - Fibular plating helps maintain alignment
- o Highest risk of nonunion w/ IMN in distal 1/3 fx (watershed area)
- o Nonunion in distal 1/3 or ¼: exchange reamed, locked nailing (dynamization destabilizes distal fragment)
- Isolated tibial shaft fracture with intact fibula: varus malunion
- Dropped hallux after tibial IMN: transient peroneal nerve neurapraxia

  → EHL weakness & sensory deficit of 1st web space.
  - o Common & often resolves by 3 months
- Proximal tibia LISS plate: highest risk of SPN injury when placing percutaneous screws at holes 11-13.
  - o vs IMN: equal time to union, increased radiation, increased OR time, increased ROH difficulty; decreased pain
- Soft tissue coverage of leg: proximal-third (gastrocnemius flap), middle-third (soleus flap), distal-third (free flap)
  - o Gastrocnemius flap: sural artery
- Distal tibia nonunion: use *posterolateral* approach; lowest rate of soft tissue complications
  - o Union rate of 75% at 10 months
- **Compartment syndrome**: compromise of venous outflow relative to arterial inflow
  - o Younger age is significant risk factor (most common w/ age groups 12-19 and 20-29)
    - Adjusted for age, diaphyseal fractures with highest risk
  - o Diagnosis:
    - ΔP (diastolic BP minus compartment pressure) <30 mmHg, or
    - Compartment pressure >30 mmHg
  - o Pediatric: AAA (agitation, anxiety & increased analgesic requirement)
  - o All tibia fx w/ CS post-fasciotomy have increased infection and nonunion rate
  - o Dual incision: SPN at risk; single incision: CPN at risk
    - No difference between infection, union, or STSG rates between single & dual

- ▪ Must take down soleus to get to deep posterior compartment
- Exertional compartment syndrome: resting P >15 mmHg, 1-minute postexercise P >30 mmHg, or 5-minute postexercise P >20 mmHg
  - o Continuous pressure measurement is more accurate than intermittent measurement
  - o Recurrence after fasciotomies is due to postsurgical fibrosis within fascial defect.

1.3.10 Pilon fracture
- 3 main fragments: anterolateral/Chaput (AITFL), posterolateral/Volkmann (PITFL), medial malleolus (deltoid)
- After pilon fracture (or any intraarticular fracture): chondrocyte cell death (apoptosis) occurs in *superficial zone* of cartilage at fracture margins
- Staged: external fixator → definitive ORIF
  - o Acute fibular fixation (with external fixator) is associated with increased postoperative complications
  - o In general, for AO/OTA C fractures (complete articular): anatomic reduction/fixation of articular surface first, then reduction/fixation of metaphysis to shaft
  - o External fixator pin care: once-daily showers & dry dressings
- Brake time after long bone diaphyseal/metaphyseal ORIF: returns to normal 9 weeks after *surgery* or 6 weeks after initiation of *weight bearing*

1.3.11 Ankle fracture
- Ok to resume driving at *6 weeks* (Ho et al, 2018) after operative treatment of ankle fx, even before weightbearing
  - o Previous studies said 9 weeks (Egol et al, 2003)
- Manual or gravity external rotation stress test to evaluate integrity of deltoid ligament (medial clear space).
  - o Abnormal if ≥5mm MCSW (NOT resting clear space)
  - o Normal: T-F clear space <5mm 1cm above joint & TF overlap of ~10mm
- First principle in treating any ankle fracture is anatomic reduction of fibula & getting fibula out to length

- o Lateral fibular plate: hardware prominence, higher intraarticular screw penetration
  - o Posterior fibular plate: peroneal tendinitis, biomechanically stronger (stiffness, strength)
- Supination adduction (SAD): buttress (antiglide) plating of medial malleolus fracture & place screws parallel to plafond
  - o Also need to address marginal impaction of anteromedial plafond
- High fibula fx: think *abduction* injury
- Lauge-Hansen (shown to be not completely accurate but still helpful for understanding some of mechanisms):
  - o SAD: 1) distal fib avulsion below level of plafond → 2) vertical medial mal
  - o SER: 1) AITFL → 2) lateral short oblique fib fx from AI to PS → 3) PITFL rupture OR PM fx → +/- transverse MM fx or deltoid ligament disruption
  - o PAb: 1) transverse MM fx or deltoid disruption → 2) transverse, comminuted fib fx *above syndesmosis*
  - o PER: 1) MM fx or deltoid disruption → 2) AITFL injury → 3) lateral short oblique or spiral fib fx from AS to PI above syndesmosis
  - o Hyperplantarflexion variant: vertical shear fx of PM tibial rim (AITFL & PITFL are intact)
    - ▪ Treatment: antiglide plating of P/PM fragments
- Posterior approach to fix displaced posterior malleolus fracture involving >25% of articular surface: interval between FHL & peroneus longus; sural nerve at risk
  - o PITFL is attached to posterior malleolus & therefore reduction/fixation of posterior malleolus (even if <25%) may be required to restore syndesmosis
- Syndesmosis: most unstable in anterior-posterior plane
  - o 4 ligaments: AITFL, PITFL, transverse tibiofibular ligament, interosseous ligament
  - o MRI is most sensitive & specific study for syndesmotic injury: *lambda sign* on coronal MRI
  - o Lateral talar shift 1mm = 42% reduction in tibiotalar contact area
  - o Most common complication after ORIF of syndesmosis is malreduction of syndesmosis

- Bosworth fracture-dislocation: fibula is entrapped behind posterolateral ridge of tibia at incisura fibularis
- Diabetic
    - Primary ORIF with multiple syndesmotic screws, immobilize for 12 weeks instead of 6 weeks
    - Nonoperative treatment poses risk for loss of reduction
    - Greatest risk factor for postoperative complications is *peripheral neuropathy*
    - If failed fixation with inadequate bone stock, proceed to arthrodesis rather than revision ORIF

1.3.12 Talus fracture
- Blood supply to talar body: PT artery → artery of *tarsal canal* (main supply) & deltoid branch of PT artery
    - Important to preserve deltoid ligament; therefore, may require medial malleolar osteotomy to access talus for ORIF
- Hawkins 1 (non-displaced): non-op w/ NWB
- Fractures of talar body vs neck are defined in relationship to *lateral process of talus*
- Blood supply to talar head/neck: artery of *tarsal sinus (ATA)*
- Comminution is usually dorsal (→ dorsal malunion) & medial (→ varus malunion)
    - Dorsal malunion: limited dorsiflexion & impingement → dorsal beak resection of talar neck
    - Varus malunion: limited subtalar eversion → medial opening wedge osteotomy of talar neck.
        - Patient walks on lateral column
- Displaced talar neck fracture: ORIF through *medial & lateral* incisions.
    - Delayed ORIF (if closed) allows for soft tissue rest & is associated w/ lower rates of infection, skin necrosis, and dehiscence *without* an increased risk of osteonecrosis
- Extruded talus fragment: clean & reimplant fragment during ORIF
- Hawkins sign: subchondral lucency on xrays (indicating bone resorption) at 6 weeks is good prognostic sign (i.e., intact vascularity)
- Posttraumatic subtalar arthritis is more common than tibiotalar arthritis
- FHL runs in groove between PM & PL talar tubercles

- Skier / snowboarder: fracture of lateral process of talus (lateral talocalcaneal ligament)
- If chronic, comminuted & symptomatic → fragment excision.

1.3.13 Calcaneus fracture
- Superomedial ("constant": because of strong ligamentous attachments—spring & deltoid ligs) fragment: FHL wraps inferior to sustentaculum tali
  - FHL is at risk when placing lateral to medial screw, especially when screw is too long → tethering of FHL → fixed, flexed hallux
- Subtalar arthritis with loss of calcaneal height (limited dorsiflexion, anterior ankle impingement): distraction bone block subtalar arthrodesis.
- If fixed & calc tuberosity is wide → subfibular impingement/peroneal tendonitis
- Most common acute, concurrent pathology is *peroneal tendon dislocation*—20% (can see on CT; often also disruption of peroneal tubercle/retinaculum avulsion)
- Better outcomes after ORIF: female, not workers' compensation, <29 years old, less comminution, sedentary jobs, Bohler's angle 0- 14°.

1.3.14 Subtalar dislocation
- Medial is more common than lateral; lateral is more often open
  - Block to reduction of medial dislocation: lateral structures (peroneal tendons, *EDB*)
  - Block to reduction of lateral dislocation: medial structures (*PT*, FHL/FDL)
- Associated with talonavicular dislocation.
- Open pantalar dislocation: most common complication is *osteonecrosis w/out collapse*—only a minority go on to collapse

1.3.15 Lisfranc injury
- Plantar ecchymoses.
- Radiographic indicators: 1) disrupted line b/w medial middle cuneiform & medial 2nd MT on AP; 2) widening b/w 1st & 2nd MT on AP; 3) dorsal

displacement of 1st or 2nd MT on lateral; 4) medial base of 4th MT not in line w/ medial cuboid on oblique; 5) disruption of medial column line (line tangential to medial navicular & medial cuneiform)

- Lisfranc ligament: medial cuneiform to base of 2nd MT
- If foot xrays initially negative, best next diagnostic study is weight-bearing foot radiographs
- Ligamentous or chronic Lisfranc: open reduction & arthrodesis of 1st to 3rd TMT joints.
  - o If chronic w/ degenerative changes: 1st->5th TMT fusion
- Bony Lisfranc: ORIF of 1st to 3rd TMT joints with screws, not K-wires.
- Primary arthrodesis vs ORIF: PA with lower cost vs ORIF
  - o Equivalent outcomes & rates of symptomatic implants, but ORIF with increased rates of hardware removal vs PA

1.3.16 Metatarsal fracture
- Operative indications: 1st MT (most of weightbearing—30-40%), multiple MT fxs, Zone 2 Jones fx in athlete

1.4 PELVIC & ACETABULAR TRAUMA

1.4.1 Adult pelvic fracture
- Mortality after isolated pelvic fx is 1-15%
  - o Anterior posterior compression (APC) is associated with hemorrhage; lateral compression (LC) is associated with head injury
  - o APCIII w/ most blood loss (more than vertical shear): shock (67%), ARDS (18%)
    - ▪ Highest mortality rate
  - o Vertical shear: shock (63%)
  - o LCIII associated w/ bowel injury (20%)
- LC injuries:
  - o LC1: impacted sacral ala fx & transverse rami fx
  - o LC2: fx of posterior tension band (unstable to IR)
    - ▪ Rami + crescent fx OR
    - ▪ Fx-dx or pure ligamentous disruption

- - LC3: "windswept pelvis"—rollover injury
    - LC one side, APC on other
- APC injuries: ER force to one or both sides OR direct impact/forceful abduction of both lower extremities
  - APC1: Rotationally stable, vertically stable
    - Isolated symphysis disruption (<2.5cm)
  - APC2: symphysis & anterior SI disruption
    - SS & ST ligaments torn (ST resists vertical translation, SS resists ER)
    - >2.5cm anterior widening
    - Rotationally unstable, vertically stable
      - APC II vs III: posterior sacroiliac ligaments are intact in APC II
  - APC3: all ligaments disrupted: rotationally & vertically unstable
    - Reduction parameters for OR: 5mm in back, 10mm in front
- Vertical shear: all ligaments disrupted; rotationally & vertically unstable; highest risk for loss of fixation
- Most common arterial injury in pelvic fx: SGA
- Angio/embolization: most common in APC & VS (20%), 2% in LC, 10% overall
  - SGA (most common overall), obturator (most common in LC), internal pudendal (bilateral = impotence)
    - All internal iliac branches
- Anterior subcutaneous pelvic fixator (INFIX)
  - Heterotopic ossification is most common complication overall
  - LFCN is most common nerve injury
  - Femoral nerve injury → loss of active knee extension
- Pelvic ex-fix
  - ASIS frame: 2 pins, 3-5cm posterior to ASIS; need *outlet OO* image
    - Helps visualize screw/Schanz pin placement along supraacetabular corridor
  - AIIS frame: 2 pins, more fluoro-dependent, more stable; increased risk of *HO & LFCN injury*
    - Line up on *inlet OO*, but can also use outlet OO
  - AIIS pins put *LFCN* at risk
  - Supraacetabular ex-fix pins w/ *less interference w/ pelvic*

surgical incisions than iliac crest pins
- Predictive of mortality: blood transfusion w/in 24h (shock), increased ISS & RTS scores, age >60, open pelvis
- Early application of pelvic compression device & CT can result in *underestimation* of injury severity.
- Percutaneous sacroiliac (SI) screw: risk to *L5 nerve* (EHL) as it runs over sacral ala
    o Inlet view: anterior-posterior screw placement
        ▪ Inlet IO: AC A-P ramus (retrograde) pin/screw placement along table of supraacetabular corridor
    o Outlet view: superior-inferior screw placement
        ▪ Outlet OO: ensures screw not in joint
        ▪ Best view to see neural foramina (and screws position relative)
    o Lateral sacral view: entry point
    o Pelvic ring injury with *vertical* fracture pattern poses greatest risk for loss of reduction of SI screw fixation
- Risk factors for deep infection after pelvic / acetabular surgery: *obesity (BMI)—#1*, leukocytosis, embolization (not just angiography alone), injury severity
- Most common urethral injury associated with pelvic fracture is *posterior urethral tear* (retrograde urethrocystogram)
- Sacral insufficiency fracture: chronic & symptomatic → percutaneous screw fixation.
- Highest risk for loss of reduction w/ vertical sacral fx
- Chronic pelvic ring instability: best assessed with alternating single-leg-stance pelvic xrays ("Flamingo" views)
- Parturition-induced pubic diastasis: nonoperative (bedrest, binder) if diastasis is <4cm
- DVT in 60% pelvic fx, PE in 27%; fatal PE in 2%
    o PPx is essential: IVC filter if closed head injury
- Sacral dysmorphism: anatomic variant in 30% to 40% of adults
    o Osseous pathways in upper sacral segment are narrower & more oblique, which precludes safe placement of transiliac-transsacral screws at S1 level
    o Safe zone for screw placement larger at S2 level in dysmorphic

patients, thus preferred level for transiliac-transsacral screw placement in this population
- ▪ Note: it is possible to safely place intraosseous iliosacral screws at S1 level if surgeon is aware of dysmorphism

1.4.2 Acetabular fracture
- Mean lateral inclination of acetabulum: 40-48°, mean anteversion 18-21°
- CT: 2mm fine cut; stability defined by intact subchondral ring in superior 10mm of acetabulum; >2mm incongruity is considered unstable
  - ○ Following ORIF, degree of displacement on post-op CT is most closely correlated with good outcomes
- Judet views: pIc-pOw
  - ○ Iliac oblique: posterior column, anterior wall
  - ○ Obturator oblique: posterior wall, anterior column
- Transverse fracture: axial CT demonstrates *vertical* fracture line
  - ○ *Elementary* acetabular fracture pattern involving both columns
- Both column fracture: complete discontinuity between articular surface & posterior ilium; spur sign (posteroinferior aspect of intact ilium) on *obturator oblique* view
- Acute ORIF during pregnancy is ok if normal fetal HR & pelvic US
- Age is independent predictor (>55yo) for inferior outcomes in patients w/ combined acetabular fx & hip dx
  - ○ Reduce hip w/in 6-12 hrs
- If anatomic reduction & no other risk factors (e.g., femoral head lesions, age >40, extended IF approach, associated fx pattern), native hip survival noted to be 80% at 20 years (Tannast et al JBJS 2012)
  - ○ Femoral head cartilage lesion is independent RF for early conversion to THA
  - ○ Patients >60yo have 30% rate of conversion to THA following acetabular ORIF
    - ▪ 75-80% 10-year implant survival following THA after acetabular fx
- Joint reactive forces of the hip are lower for *TDWB* than NWB
  - ○ *Posterosuperior* aspect of acetabulum experiences highest

forces.
- o *Passive hip abduction* produces lowest JRF (in addition to TDWB)
- o Greatest JRF at hip when rising from chair on affected leg
- If indicated, perform ORIF early (<5 days) rather than late (>10-14 days) because easier to mobilize & reduce fracture fragments.
  - o Surgery after *3 weeks* associated with difficulty w/ reduction & poor outcomes
- Approaches
  - o Anterior: ilioinguinal, iliofemoral, Stoppa
  - o Posterior: Kocher-Langenbeck
  - o Combined: extended iliofemoral
    - ▪ Extended iliofemoral approach: highest risk for HO
  - o Recovery of post-op hip strength portends good functional outcomes regardless of which approach used
- Percutaneous ramus/column screw fixation
  - o Inlet iliac oblique view: anteroposterior screw placement in pubic ramus (avoid intra-pelvic screw penetration).
  - o Inlet obturator oblique view: ensure screw placement within inner & outer tables of ilium
  - o Outlet obturator oblique view: ensure placement outside of joint (superior inferior screw placement)
- Corona mortis: anastomosis of epigastric (branch of external iliac) & obturator (branch of internal iliac) vessels
  - o Ligated during Stoppa approach.
- Roof-arc angles: drawn on AP, OO, and IO views → vertical & 45deg
  - o If fx w/in arc: unstable; outside of arc: stable
  - o NOT applicable to ABC or PC fx as no intact portion of acetabulum to reference
  - o Vrahas et al: roof arc angles less than these are unstable & need fixation:
    - ▪ Medial RAA 45°, Anterior RAA 25°, Posterior RAA 70°
- Non-op if <2mm displacement & no instability: TTWB x 6-8 weeks
- 5 elementary types
  - o Posterior wall
    - ▪ <20%: non-op; 40-50%: fixation
    - ▪ Common to do dynamic EUA w/ OO views on fluoro w/

posterior directed force—if unstable: ORIF
- Opening of *medial clear space* is indicative of instability during EUA
  - High-energy deceleration mechanism w/ posterior hip dx is associated w/ thoracic aortic injury (8%)
  - Posterior column
    - SG A/V/N injury common
    - Intact iliopectineal line, disrupted ilioischial line
  - Anterior column: ilioinguinal approach
    - Can also perc if minimally displaced
  - Anterior wall
  - Transverse: both columns involved & thus both lines (II and IP) disrupted
    - Next step to eval obturator ring—if intact: transverse or transverse w/ associated PW
    - CT w/ vertical fx line running A-P
- 5 associated types
  - Transverse-PW: most common of associated
    - Disrupted II & IP lines w/ intact obturator ring
    - *Highest incidence of nerve injury*
  - Both column
    - IP & II disruption
    - "Spur sign" on OO (intact posterior column to sciatic buttress)
    - *No attached articular surface to innominate bone*
  - T-shaped
    - Both columns + fx of obturator ring
    - Need combined A + P approach
  - Anterior column posterior hemitransverse
    - II, IP & obturator ring disrupted
    - Most common in elderly
      - Another variant most common in elderly is "AC + medial wall"
  - PC-PW
    - Only associated fx type w/ intact IP line (both columns not affected, only posterior)
- HO after acetabular ORIF: most common in *gluteus minimus*

- Nerve injury in acetabular fx: common peroneal branch of sciatic (53%) > complete sciatic (25%) > LFCN (16%)

1.4.3 Pelvic & acetabular approaches
- Extended IF: highest risk of HO (and K-L)
  - o Lowest risk of HO: ilioinguinal
  - o Treat HO w/ indomethacin x 5 wks vs low-dose radiation
- Timing to good anatomic reduction is key to good outcome
- ONFH happens in 7-8% acetabular fx, 18% of posterior wall fx-dx
- Anterior/ilioinguinal
  - o Good for AW, AC, both column fx
    - AC can be fixed percutaneously if minimal displacement
  - o Access to anterior SIJ, internal iliac fossa, crest, sup pubic ramus/symphysis, quadrilateral surface
  - o At risk: femoral nerve & LFCN (L2-3), *corona mortis (6.2cm from pubic symphysis—range of 3-9cm)*
  - o Medial window: medial to EIA/V
    - Access to pubic rami, indirect to IIF & anterior SIJ
  - o Middle window: between EIA/V & iliopectineal fascia
    - Access to pelvic brim, QP, portion of SPR
  - o Lateral window: lateral to IP fascia
    - Access to QP, SIJ, iliac wing
- Modified Stoppa
  - o For medialization of quadrilateral plate & access to supraacetabular fx segments
    - "Medial wall" fx
  - o Also need to watch out for corona mortis (but less at risk compared to ilioinguinal)
  - o Lateral window during Stoppa w/ retractor on sacrum: L5 nerve root at risk
- Posterior/Kocher-Langenbeck
  - o Good for PW and PC, T, & T-type fx
  - o Higher risk of HO than ilioinguinal
  - o At risk: sciatic nerve (most commonly 2/2 errant retractor placement; 2-10%)
    - Decrease w/ hip extension, knee flexion

- o Limited access to supraacetabular fx segments
- o MFCA is at deep/inferior aspect of QF
  - ▪ Obturator externus protects MFCA above QF
- o Greater sciatic notch
  - ▪ Above piriformis: SG A/V/N
  - ▪ Below piriformis: "POPSIQ"
    - • Pudendal nerve, Obturator internus (nerve to), PCN of thigh, Sciatic nerve, IG A/V/N, Quad femoris (nerve to)
- • Extended IF
  - o Direct visualization of both columns & articular surface: T, T-type, both column
  - o Highest risk of HO
  - o Best of nonunion and malunion (delayed recon)
  - o Associated with early conversion to THA (risk factor)
    - ▪ Other risk factors for early THA: initial displacement >20mm, age >40, incongruent acetabular roof

1.4.4. Sacral fracture
- • S2-5 redundancy: bowel/bladder function (voluntary sphincter contraction), perianal sensation, bulbocavernosus reflex
- • Presence of neuro deficit is most important determinant of outcome
  - o Displacement confers increased risk of neuro injury
- • Denis classification
  - o Zone 1: 20% risk of nerve injury (L5); lateral to foramina
  - o Zone 2: at foramina; 30% risk of nerve injury
    - ▪ Shear component at Zone 2 is highly unstable
  - o Zone 3: medial to foramina; 60% risk of nerve injury
- • U-type: needs CT imaging
  - o Possible spino-pelvic dissociation
  - o Treatment: vertical fx → SI screws vs posterior plating
    - ▪ Highly unstable: combined iliosacral + lumbopelvic fixation ("triangular osteosynthesis"; strongest)

DOMAIN 2: SHOULDER & ELBOW

2.1 SHOULDER

2.1.1 Glenohumeral ligaments

Ligament	Restraints
SGHL	Inferior translation at $0°$ abduction (neutral rotation)
MGHL	Anterior & posterior translation at $45°$ abduction
IGHL	Anterior band: anterior & inferior translation at $90°$ abduction & maximum ER Posterior band: posterior translation at $90°$ flexion & IR
CHL	Resists posterior translation when flexed, adducted, IR

- Buford complex (congenital variant): no anterosuperior labrum (bare area), cordlike MGHL
- Anterior band of IGHL attaches to anterior labrum → Bankart lesion
- Posterior band of IGHL attaches to posterior labrum → reverse Bankart (posterior labral tear)
- Release of CA ligament during arthroscopy leads to anterior/inferior translation of glenohumeral joint
- Biceps tendon attaches to superior labrum → SLAP tear.
  - o Insertion is 70% PS, 25% at 12 o'clock, rarely anterior
- Rotator interval
  - o Boundaries: supraspinatus tendon (superior), subscapularis tendon (inferior), coracoid (medial), transverse humeral ligament (lateral; stabilizes LHB in groove)
  - o Content: SGHL, coracohumeral ligament (CHL), long head of biceps tendon
    - ▪ Rotator cable is an extension of CHL; thickened fibers at insertion of IS & SS (perpendicular to)
    - ▪ During arthroscopic release of interval, landmark for complete release is visualization of *CA ligament* superficially

2.1.2 Anterior shoulder dislocation & instability
- Age at time of dislocation (<40 years) is strongest predictor of redislocation

- o   Dislocate / unstable with shoulder in abduction & ER
- Most common injury with patients >40yo following dx: rotator cuff tear
- Bankart lesion (anteroinferior labral tear) may be associated with avulsion of anterior inferior glenohumeral ligament at humeral insertion (HAGL lesion)
  - o   Anterior band of IGHL attaches to anterior labrum (Bankart lesion) & proximal humerus (HAGL lesion)
- Recurrent instability: arthroscopic Bankart repair & capsular shift
  - o   Arthroscopic Bankart repair w/ *better ROM* but otherwise equal outcomes
  - o   Attritional glenoid bone loss is a risk factor for recurrent instability
    - ▪   Glenoid bone loss is best assessed with 3D CT reconstruction
  - o   Latarjet (coracoid transfer) if glenoid deficiency is >20-25%; risk to musculocutaneous (most common) & axillary nerves.
    - ▪   MSCT nerve with instrumentation around conjoint, axillary usually during graft fixation
    - ▪   Good outcomes (low recurrent instability & reoperation rates) but return to sport shown to be no earlier than 3 months
- Remplissage procedure: transfer posterior capsule & infraspinatus tendon into large Hill-Sachs lesion (posterosuperior humeral head)
  - o   Large Hill-Sachs lesion (>25-40%) will engage with glenoid: catching sensation when arm is 90° abduction & 90° ER
    - ▪   Hill-Sachs lesion >40% requires bone grafting
  - o   After surgery, avoid adduction with shoulder forward flexed to 90° because this will stress the posterior myocapsulodesis

2.1.3 Posterior shoulder dislocation & instability
- Dislocate / unstable with shoulder in flexion, adduction & IR
  - o   Seizure & electrocution → arm locked in *IR* (i.e., lack of ER)
  - o   Subscapularis is most important at preventing posterior subluxation
- Posteroinferior labral tear (reverse Bankart)
  - o   Posterior load & shift test or Jerk test reproduces pain & instability
  - o   Kim's lesion: incomplete & concealed avulsion of

posteroinferior labrum
- If fails nonoperative treatment → arthroscopic posterior labral repair & capsular shift
  - To protect repair after surgery, avoid adduction with shoulder flexed at shoulder level for first 3 weeks
- Reverse Hill-Sachs lesion >25-40% (anteromedial humeral head): subscapularis transfer (McLaughlin) or lesser tuberosity transfer (modified McLaughlin)

2.1.4 Inferior shoulder dislocation (luxatio erecta)
- Shoulder fixed in *abduction*

2.1.5 Multidirectional instability (MDI)
- Instability in ≥2 planes (anterior, posterior or inferior)
- If fails *6 months* of PT (dynamic stabilization program) → capsular shift & plication, closure of rotator interval
  - Closure of rotator interval will limit shoulder ER with arm at 0° abduction
  - Inferior plication: axillary nerve is 1cm away at 6 o'clock position; can try *abduction, ER, and traction* to pull out of way
  - Avoid thermal capsulorrhaphy because of chondrolysis

2.1.6 Parsonage-Turner syndrome
- Also known as idiopathic brachial neuritis or neuralgic amyotrophy
- Intense shoulder / upper extremity pain, multifocal weakness (patchy paresis), fatty atrophy on MRI, EMG with denervation & reinnervation potentials
- Treatment: observation

2.1.7 Thoracic outlet syndrome
- Compression of brachial plexus (→ paresthesias & sensorimotor deficits of upper extremity), subclavian artery (→ cool, pallor upper extremity) or subclavian vein (→ swelling, discoloration of upper extremity)
  - Symptoms occur with overhead activities
  - Common causes: hypertrophy of scalene muscles, Pancoast tumor, cervical rib

2.1.8 Quadrilateral (quadrangular) space syndrome
- Boundaries: teres minor, teres major, long head of triceps, humerus
  - Content: axillary nerve, PCHA
- Compression in thrower is worse during late cocking/early acceleration (maximum shoulder ABD & ER)

2.1.9 Glenohumeral arthritis
- Osteoarthritis pattern: eccentric glenoid wear (posterior glenoid wear & posterior humeral head subluxation)
  - 5-10% w/ RCTs
- Inflammatory arthritis (e.g., RA) pattern: concentric glenoid wear → medialization of GH joint
  - 25-50% w/ RCTs
- TSA has lower revision/reoperation rate compared to hemiarthroplasty
  - After TSA, most common reason for revision is loosening of implant (glenoid >>> humeral component)
- Development of OA is closely related to # of previous dislocations (if any)
  - Glenoid bone loss is also a risk factor
  - Best study to eval glenoid bone loss is CT w/ 3D recon
- Glenohumeral dysplasia secondary to unresolved brachial plexus palsy causes glenoid retroversion, posterior subluxation of HH & HH flattening

2.1.10 Shoulder replacement
- Hemiarthroplasty
  - Younger patients w/ intact CA arch, anterior 1/3 deltoid.
  - Outcomes: improved pain but will not improve function (40-70° elevation).
- In general, for failed hemiarthroplasty or progressive arthritis of glenoid, convert to TSA
  - For failed TSA, convert to rTSA
    - rTSA: center of rotation is moved *medially* & *inferiorly* → decreases deltoid abduction force & joint load
    - Dislocated rTSA: CR & immobilization under general anesthesia

- Latissimus dorsi transfer can help improve external rotation
  - If loss of active ER (positive Hornblower's), should consider concomitant LD transfer with rTSA
    - Anterior approach for LD transfer: radial nerve passes anterior to tendon & is at risk
    - Posterior approach: axillary nerve
    - Minimize risk to radial nerve w/ instrumentation proximal to inferior edge of LD tendon
- TSA: thickness of humeral head is ~70% its radius of curvature
  - Humeral head center of rotation (COR) is ~4mm posterior & ~8mm medial to center of humeral intramedullary canal
  - For TSA, if there is eccentric glenoid wear & humeral head subluxation → graft of posterior glenoid to address glenoid deficiency & eccentric glenoid reaming to restore native glenoid version
  - Metal-backed glenoids w/ higher rate of failure than all-poly, pegged glenoids better than keeled, cemented w/ lower revision rate than uncemented → remember "pegged poly cemented"
  - Most common failure with anatomic TSA & rTSA is *glenoid component loosening*
    - Unique to rTSA is scapular notching (most common) AFTER glenoid loosening), acromial stress fx (2nd most common) & dislocation (3rd most common) but dx is NOT related to condition of RC
  - Neck cut too low—cut into RC
- Lesser tuberosity osteotomy: limit ER to 30° x 6 weeks to protect repair
- PMI is 5.6cm below top of implant; GT should be 5-8mm below top of implant
- Use LHB for tuberosity reconstruction; in absence of this, use anterior aspect of prosthesis; can also look for PM insertion since it runs inferior to LHB
- Deltopectoral approach: need to identify & cauterize anterior humeral circumflex vessels (three sisters)
- rTSA dx usually when pushing out of chair via active subscap for IR
- Risk factors for loosening: 1) glenoid retroversion >10°, 2) posterior HH subluxation on axillary, 3) excessive reaming, 4) superior tilt, 5) Walch B2 (biconcave) glenoid

44

- *P. acnes* is most common organism responsible for PJI after shoulder replacement surgery
    - Gram-positive aerotolerant anaerobic Bacillus.
    - Risk factor for infection after shoulder arthroplasty: *male gender (especially young males)*, elevated BMI
    - *Penicillin* w/ lowest MIC (best); can also use Vanc or Zosyn
- TSA pearls
    - Don't overstuff (increased JRF), avoid valgus stem
    - Stem in 25-45° retroversion
    - Glenoid retroversion 15-20°: eccentric reaming; if >20°: bone grafting (can also consider rTSA if persistent concern for instability)
    - Glenoid: uncemented w/ increased rate of loosening
        - Conforming: more stable but increased rim stress & radiolucencies
        - Non-conforming: increased poly wear

2.1.11 Avascular necrosis of humeral head
- #1 trauma; #2 cause is steroids → also check hip XR
- Most common site on XR is superior middle portion of humeral head
- Treatment
    - Precollapse: core decompression
    - Collapse: hemiarthroplasty (TSA if glenoid changes)

2.1.12 Subacromial & subcoracoid impingement
- Subacromial impingement: Type 3 (hooked) acromion, os acromiale
    - Diagnose os acromiale w/ axillary XR
    - Treat via fusion f/b acromioplasty (if acute resection → deltoid dysfunction)
- Subcoracoid impingement: pain over anterior shoulder that is worse w/ FADIR
    - Normal CH distance adducted: 8.7mm; flexed: 6.7mm
        - Any CHD ≤6 is abnormal
    - Treatment: if non-op fails → coracoplasty w/ goal of 7mm minimum distance b/w coracoid & subscap +/- subscap repair

2.2 ELBOW

2.2.1 Anatomy & mechanics
- Kocher interval: between anconeus & ECU
- MCL is primary restraint to valgus at 30-120°; anterior MCL attaches 18mm distal to tip of coronoid
- Accessory lateral portal w/ elbow scope puts PIN at risk

2.2.2 Elbow stiffness
- Flexion contracture >30° or flexion <130°: static progressive elbow splinting
- If fails nonoperative treatment, capsular release with possible release of *posterior* oblique bundle of MCL; posterior bundle is tight in flexion
    - o Ulnar nerve decompression if symptomatic preoperatively
    - o Open vs arthroscopic contracture release: avoid arthroscopy in obese patients with prior elbow surgery
- Young laborer with advanced osteoarthritis at radiocapitellar & ulnohumeral joints who is symptomatic (e.g., stiffness, pain): osteophyte resection & capsular release.

2.2.3 Ulnohumeral arthritis
- Active patient with minimal radiocapitellar arthritis: arthroscopic ulnohumeral arthroplasty (fenestration of olecranon fossa, osteophyte debridement, remove loose bodies, capsular release).
    - o Also called osteocapsular arthroplasty (OCA)
    - o Ideal candidate with *stable elbow*, *painless mid-arc ROM*, but stiffness due to osteophytes & mild-moderate arthritic changes
- Elbow arthroscopy portals/nerve risk
    - o Proximal AM portal: MABCN closest (1mm)
    - o AM (direct medial) portal: MABCN closest (1mm)
    - o Proximal AL portal: Radial n (10mm) & PABCN (0-14mm; variable)
    - o AL portal: PIN closest (2-10mm; variable)
    - o Proximal PL portal: unlikely injury; medial & PABCN >2cm away

2.2.4 Osteochondritis dissecans (OCD) of elbow
- Usually at *capitellum*: painful catching / clicking / locking
- Posterolateral elbow impingement: secondary to radiocapitellar plica; think throwing athletes & golfers; painful snap w/ pronation, valgus load, and passive flexion but no instability or apprehension

2.2.5 Total elbow replacement
- Best outcome for rheumatoid arthritis
- Triceps reflecting technique (M → L) associated w/ loss of extension strength
- Best TER systems are semiconstrained (linked)

DOMAIN 3: HAND

3.1 BASICS

3.1.1 Anatomy

- Order of ossification of carpals: capitate (1-3 mos), hamate (2-4 mos), triquetrum (2-3y), lunate (2-4y), scaphoid (4-6y), trapezium (4-6y), trapezoid (4-6y), pisiform (8-12y)
- Ulnar artery supplies superficial palmar arch while radial artery supplies deep palmar arch
  - o In digit, digital artery is dorsal to digital nerve
- Radioscaphocapitate (RSC) ligament is the radial most extrinsic ligament of wrist
- Dorsal MCP dislocation: volar plate interposition can prevent reduction
- Wrist arthroscopy
  - o Initial (3,4) portal placement is 1cm directly distal to Lister tubercle between EPL & EDC tendons
  - o 6R or 6U portal: dorsal sensory branch of ulnar nerve at risk
  - o 1,2 portal: superficial sensory branch of radial nerve & radial artery at risk

Receptor	Function
Free nerve ending	Pain (nociception)
Meissner corpuscle	Touch, pressure (dynamic)
Pacinian corpuscle	Deep pressure & vibration
Merkel cell	Sustained touch & pressure (static)
Ruffini ending	Skin stretch
Golgi tendon organ	Muscle length & tension proprioception

3.1.2 Dorsal hand compartments

Compartment	Tendon	Pathology
1	EPB, APL	De Quervain's tenosynovitis • Postpartum; pain near radial styloid; +Finkelstein test • Surgery: incision of first dorsal wrist compartment at *dorsal* edge
2	ECRL, ECRB	Intersection syndrome • Rower; pain 5cm proximal to wrist joint
3	EPL	
4	EIP, EDC, PIN	
5	EDM	Vaughan-Jackson syndrome • Rheumatoid wrist: DRUJ instability causes volar carpal subluxation → attritional rupture of digital extensor tendons from ulnar to radial (EDM is first to rupture)
6	ECU	Snapping ECU • Due to attenuation/tear of ECU subsheath (part of TFCC) • ECU subluxates with forearm supination

3.2 BONY INJURIES

3.2.1 Scaphoid fracture
- Mechanism: fall onto outstretched wrist in extension & radial deviation
  - Highest load transmission through radioscaphoid articulation when wrist is extended
- Waist fracture is most common in adult, distal pole most common in pediatric
- Dorsal carpal branch (of radial artery) supplies scaphoid from distal to proximal (retrograde flow)

49

- Thumb spica cast if nondisplaced or if concern for scaphoid fracture despite normal radiographs
  - XR for scaphoid fx more sensitive w/ wrist extension & ulnar deviation
- Any displacement → ORIF
  - Proximal pole fracture: dorsal approach.
    - Usually worst outcome because of blood supply (retrograde flow)
  - Waist or distal pole fracture, or if there's humpback deformity: volar approach
  - Long screw down *central* axis of scaphoid
    - Direct visualization is best way to ensure proper screw seating below subchondral bone.
    - Perc associated w/ intra-articular penetration
- Nonunion in young patient: revision ORIF with vascularized *medial femoral condyle* graft
  - Nonunion manifests typically as volar collapse w/ humpback deformity
  - Obtain CT scan along axis of scaphoid to assess union
  - Note: rate of success w/ any revision & bone grafting is about 66-75%
  - Salvage for failed reconstruction is excision of distal pole
    - Absolute contraindication to this is *SLIL injury* as this will precipitate instability & arthrosis

3.2.2 Scaphoid nonunion advanced collapse (SNAC)

Stage	Involvement	Operative treatment
I	Arthrosis between scaphoid & radial styloid	Radial styloidectomy
II	Arthrosis between scaphoid & capitate	PRC, four-corner fusion, wrist arthrodesis
III	Periscaphoid arthrosis +/- lunocapitate joint	PRC, four-corner fusion, wrist arthrodesis

- Distal pole flexes & proximal pole follows lunate into extension
- Radiolunate joint is usually not involved

- PRC vs 4-corner fusion: largely equivalent but slightly better grip & R-U deviation with 4CF
  - PRC w/ decreased grip & wrist motion; avoid if capitate head degenerative changes
  - 4CF: 60% wrist motion & 80% grip strength retained

3.2.3 Carpal fracture
- Hook of hamate fracture
  - Chronic nonunion fracture of hook of hamate can cause rupture of small finger FDP & ulnar neuropathy (hook of hamate forms radial border of Guyon canal)
    - Acute fracture: immobilization
    - Chronic fracture or nonunion: excision of fracture fragment
  - Obtain *carpal tunnel* radiograph to assess (best).
    - Can also use supinated lateral or lateral w/ wrist in radial deviation + thumb abduction
- Pisiform fracture
  - Pisiform is located within FCU tendon
  - Acute fracture: immobilization
  - Chronic fracture or nonunion: excision of fracture fragment

3.2.4 Metacarpal fracture

Non-op parameters	Shaft angulation	Shortening	Neck angulation
IF, LF	10-20	2-5mm	10-15
RF	30	2-5mm	30-40
SF	40	2-5mm	50-60

- Important for non-op: no rotational deformity
- 5th MC fx: if no rotational deformity & <70 neck/head angulation: evaluation & management, no follow-up needed
- Tension through *deep transverse intermetacarpal ligament* is primary restraint against shortening of metacarpal shaft fx (greater effect in non-border digits)
- Shaft: CRPP or ORIF if intraarticular, rotational malalignment or multiple MC fractures

51

- o Oblique fracture pattern: interfragmentary fixation is preferred over plate fixation
- Thumb metacarpal base fracture
  - o Bennett fracture: intraarticular fracture of volar lip of metacarpal base
    - Volar oblique ligament holds fragment in place
    - Deformity due to pull from AddP (supination-adduction on shaft; ulnar n), EPL and APL (proximal, dorsal, radial force on shaft; PIN).
    - Reduce with traction, palmar abduction, and pronation.
  - o Rolando fracture: comminuted intraarticular fracture of metacarpal base
- Thumb CMC dislocation
  - o Usually dorsal due to disruption of dorsoradial ligament
  - o Anterior oblique ("volar beak") ligament is primary stabilizer of thumb CMC; originates at base of thumb & inserts into volar tubercle of trapezium
  - o Dorsal MP dx: dorsal approach if need to open because less risk of injury to neurovascular structures and better access to any articular fx
- SF CMC dislocation: usually axial load, use *30° pronated lateral* XR

3.2.5 Phalanx fracture dislocation
- Most important determinant of outcome is maintenance of alignment of middle phalanx on lateral view
- Dorsal PIP dislocation: *volar plate* interposition can prevent closed reduction
  - o Volar plate disruption → swan neck deformity
  - o Most common fracture is volar lip of P2
    - <40% joint involved or joint is stable after reduction: dorsal extension block splint with active flexion & extension
    - >40% joint involved or joint is unstable after reduction: CRPP vs ORIF
- Volar PIP dislocation: central slip disruption → boutonniere deformity
  - o In fracture-dislocation, if <40% joint involved or joint is stable after reduction: splint in extension

- ▪ >40% joint involved or joint is unstable after reduction: CRPP vs ORIF
      - ▪ If volar base of middle phalanx is comminuted in young patient → hemi-hamate arthroplasty
- For dorsal/volar PIP fx-dx: if comminuted, can also consider dynamic ex-fix
- Dorsal DIP dislocation: *volar plate* interposition can prevent closed reduction

3.3 TENDINOUS & LIGAMENTOUS INJURIES

3.3.1 Tendon rupture
- Blood supply
    - o Distal to A5: interosseous & VLB
    - o A5: VLB
        - ▪ Disruption of VLB blood supply w/ retraction to PIP
    - o PIP/volar plate: VLP
        - ▪ Disruption of VLP blood supply w/ retraction proximal to PIP
- Days 0-5: inflammatory; 5-28: fibroblastic; 28+: remodeling
    - o Weakest at days 6-12 following repair
- Acute: primary repair (w/in 2 weeks; no later than 3 weeks)
    - o 4-strand core repair (placed 1cm away from edge) with 6-0 epitendinous suture
        - ▪ Avoid locking suture
        - ▪ Aim to place dorsally
    - o Surgery under local anesthesia allows assessment of tendon gliding intraoperatively & also allows correct tensioning
- Chronic: silastic tendon implant (silicone tube) with staged reconstruction ("2-stage").
    - o Most common complication: flexion contracture due to overtightening of graft
- Partial flexor tendon (<60% tendon width) laceration without triggering: early ROM
    - o If there is triggering: trim frayed edges
        - ▪ Avoid tenorrhaphy
    - o If >60%: 4-0 core repair w/ 6-0 epitendinous sutures

- FDS rupture in Zone II: repairing only 1 slip improves gliding (compared to repairing 2 slips)
- If FDP too short or advanced too much (>1cm): quadrigia
- Post-op protocols: low stress, low excursion
  - Kleinert: dorsal blocking splint in wrist 45° extension; active extension & passive flexion (rubber bands)
  - Duran: other hand to passively flex hand, then actively extend digits & flex wrist

3.3.2 Trigger finger
- Pulley: A2 & A4 are most important & prevent bowstringing
  - A1, A3 & A5 pulleys overlie MCPJ, PIPJ & DIPJ, respectively
  - Can cut A4 & vent A2 if needed
- Adult trigger thumb
  - Release A1 pulley
  - Do not release oblique pulley (most important) → bowstringing of FPL

3.3.3 Jersey finger
- FDP avulsion → DIP extension at rest compared to other digits
- FDP injury: loss of normal digital cascade as wrist is passively flexed & extended
- Direct repair if acute, two-stage reconstruction if chronic
  - Quadrigia effect results if FDP is functionally shortened >1cm
    - FDP to long, ring & small fingers share common muscle belly → shortening one FDP tendon leads to flexion lag (loss of full flexion) to other two FDP tendons

3.3.4 Lumbrical plus
- Lumbricals originate from FDP (just proximal to A1) & insert on *radial* lateral band; lumbrical 1 & 2 (median nerve) are unipennate; lumbrical 3 & 4 (ulnar nerve) are bipennate
  - All flex MPs & extend PIP and DIP
  - When FDP is functionally impaired, firing of FDP (i.e., attempt to flex finger) causes pull on lumbricals, ultimately leading to *paradoxical* extension of finger instead (at PIP/DIPs).

- Causes of functional deficit of FDP—loss of distal FDP tethering: FDP transection / avulsion, DIP amputation, or FDP reconstruction with *long* graft (excessive FDP lengthening).
  - o Treatment: repair or (if chronic) release

3.3.5 Mallet finger
- Disruption of terminal extensor tendon → DIP flexion at rest compared to other digits
- Nondisplaced fracture or soft tissue injury only: extension splinting of DIPJ
  - o Nonoperative injury heals with loss of terminal extension without functional deficits
- CRPP or ORIF for large bony mallet with volar subluxation of distal phalanx
- Mallet finger can cause swan neck deformity
- Seymour fracture: through physeal plate of distal phalanx in peds
  - o Subluxated nail plate & interposition of nail matrix often block anatomic reduction
  - o Acute (<24hrs): CR + antibiotics ok (if stable reduction)
  - o Chronic (>24hrs): surgical I&D, fixation, IV abx

3.3.6 Swan neck deformity
- Most often caused by volar plate injury/attenuation → PIP hyperextension, DIP flexion.
- Causes: mallet finger, FDS rupture (unopposed PIP extension), dorsal PIP dx (more common than volar)
- Treatment: VP advancement +/- FDS tenodesis or CS release

3.3.7 Central slip disruption (Boutonniere deformity)
- Central slip normally helps EDC extend PIP
  - o Disruption of central slip causes volar migration of lateral bands → *PIP flexion & DIP extension* due to unopposed pull of lumbricals
- Elson test: with PIPJ flexed to 90°, attempted extension of PIPJ against resistance leads to DIP hyperextension
- Acute injury: extension splinting of PIP x 6 weeks or CS repair

- Open or fx: fix, avulsion: repair
- Chronic: CS reconstruction +/- triangular ligament reconstruction
  - Triangular ligament prevents volar subluxation of lateral bands (attenuation of this & thus volar subluxation of lateral bands with CS injury)
  - Transverse retinacular ligament: prevents dorsal subluxation of lateral bands
- Chronic Boutonniere: ORL contracture
  - ORL links PIP & DIP in motion via lateral bands (from volar A2 to dorsal extensor mechanism past PIP)

3.3.8 Carpal instability
- Carpal kinematics
  - Flexion—40% RC, 60% MC (midcarpal)
  - Extension—66% RC, 33% MC
  - Radial deviation—10% RC, 90% MC
  - Ulnar deviation—50% RC, 50% MC
- Carpal extrinsic ligaments
  - Volar (generally stronger than dorsal)
    - RSC: at risk of injury w/ large radial styloid
      - Acts as sling to support waist of scaphoid
      - Preserve w/ PRC! Prevents ulnar drift of carpus
    - RL: aka RLT or volar RL ligament; short and long
      - Counteracts ulnar-distal translocation of lunate
      - Abnormal in Madelung's
    - Deltoid ligaments: originate on Tq and scaphoid, converge on capitate
    - RSL (ligament of Testut & Kuenz)
      - Only functions as NV conduit
    - Space of Poirier: floor of carpal tunnel near proximal capitate b/w RSC and LRL
      - Area of weakness increases w/ extension, decreases w/ flexion
      - Lunate dx—lunate escapes into this space
      - Perilunate dx—allows distal carpal row to

separate from lunate (lunate stays in place while carpus dx around it)

- o Dorsal
  - ▪ Ligaments converge on triquetrum.
  - ▪ For VISI deformity, RT (aka DRC) must be disrupted w/ LT
  - ▪ DIC ("dorsal intercarpal): runs from capitate to Tq
  - ▪ RT (aka DRC): runs from distal radius to Tq
  - ▪ Smaller dorsal ligaments: RS, RL
- Perilunate dissociation
  - o Usually a high-energy injury w/ wrist in extension-ulnar deviation
  - o Mayfield's classification (spectrum): 1) SL disruption → 2) lunocapitate disruption → 3) LT disruption ("perilunate") → 4) lunate dislocation from lunate fossa (usually volar; associated w/ median nerve compression)
    - ▪ AP XR: "piece of pie" sign (lunate-capitate overlap)
    - ▪ Lateral XR: "spilled teacup" sign (lunate)
  - o Lunate dislocation causing acute carpal tunnel syndrome → emergent closed vs open reduction
  - o If lunate dislocates volarly into carpal tunnel, combined dorsal & volar approaches are preferred
    - ▪ Short radiolunate ligament is usually intact & holds lunate in place while rest of carpus dx around it
  - o Chronic dislocation: proximal row carpectomy.
    - ▪ If fails PRC → wrist arthrodesis
- Scapholunate ligament deficiency → dorsal intercalated segmental instability (DISI)
  - o Fall w/ wrist extension & ulnar deviation
  - o Degenerative SL injuries in 50% >80yo; 10-30% intra-articular DRFx
  - o Lunate tilted *dorsally* (lunate extension)
  - o SL angle >60, ALWAYS pathologic
  - o Terry Thomas sign: scapholunate diastasis >3mm with clenched fist radiograph
  - o Acute tear → SL repair; chronic tear → SL reconstruction

- o SLIL
  - ▪ Dorsal component is strongest & thickest, volar component prevents rotation
  - ▪ Disruption results in lunate extension when scaphoid flexes (DISI)
- Lunotriquetral ligament deficiency → volar intercalated segmental instability (VISI)
  - o Fall w/ wrist extension & radial deviation
  - o Lunate tilted *volarly* (lunate flexion)—scaphoid induces lunate to flex while Tq extends.
  - o SL angle <30, may not be pathologic
  - o Requires disruption of LT *and* RT (radiotriquetral aka dorsal radiocarpal ligament)
  - o LT ligament
    - ▪ Volar component is strongest & thickest, dorsal component confers rotational stability
    - ▪ Disruption results in lunate flexion w/ scaphoid normally aligned, Tq extends (VISI)
- Wrist extension increases pressure on scaphoid facet, decreases pressure on lunate facet (of distal radius)

3.3.9 Scapholunate advanced collapse (SLAC)

Stage	Involvement	Surgical options
I	Arthritis between scaphoid & radial styloid	Radial styloidectomy & scaphoid stabilization; PIN/AIN neurectomy
II	Arthritis between scaphoid & entire radius (vs periscaphoid arthrosis in SNAC)	Proximal row carpectomy, scaphoid excision & 4-corner fusion
III	Arthritis between capitate & lunate	Scaphoid excision & 4-corner fusion; radiocarpal arthrodesis

- Radiolunate joint is usually not involved
- During PRC, preserving RSC ligament is essential to prevent ulnar subluxation (CI if compromised).

- PRC is contraindicated if there is capitolunate arthritis (stage III)
- Advantage to PRC: no need for as much immobilization, no risk of nonunion or hardware complications

3.3.10 Gamekeeper's (or skier's) thumb
- Stener lesion: avulsed UCL is displaced above adductor aponeurosis → adductor aponeurosis blocks reduction of UCL
- Proper UCL: valgus stability when thumb MCPJ is at 30° of flexion
- Accessory UCL: valgus stability when thumb MCPJ is at full extension
- Acute tear (→ repair) vs chronic tear (→ reconstruction)

3.3.11 Sagittal band rupture
- Most common is radial SB of LF
- Leads to dislocation of extensor tendon especially during MCP flexion with wrist flexed
  - Radial sagittal band ruptures more often → tendon dislocates ulnarly (away from injured side)
- Acute injury: extension splinting of MCPJ
- Chronic injury or athlete: direct repair if possible, otherwise extensor centralization procedure
- Rheumatoid hand: sagittal band dysfunction leads to ulnar deviation of digits

3.3.12 Claw hand (intrinsic minus)
- MCP hyperextension (strong EDC) & PIP/DIP flexion (strong FDP & FDS)
- Due to ulnar or median nerve palsy (e.g., Volkmann's ischemic contracture, CMT-PMP22)
- Extrinsic tightness: more PIP flexion with MCP extension than with MCP flexion (would be tough to flex PIPs w/ MPs flexed because tightness puts extrinsics more on stretch)
  - Due to extensor tendon adhesions

3.3.13 Intrinsic plus
- Weak extrinsics & spastic intrinsics → MCP flexion & PIP/DIP extension

- Intrinsic tightness: less PIP flexion with MCP extended then with MCP flexed (because intrinsics stretched)
  - Bunnell test ddx between intrinsic and extrinsic tightness.
  - Therapy, distal intrinsic releases

3.4 VASCULAR CONDITIONS

3.4.1 Hypothenar hammer syndrome
- Arteriography is gold standard for diagnosis & surgical planning
- Ulnar artery thrombosis: observation
- Ulnar artery aneurysm ("corkscrew" artery): excision & reconstruction

3.4.2 Raynaud's disease or syndrome
- Raynaud's disease: idiopathic
- Raynaud's phenomenon or syndrome: known underlying cause
- Cold temperature or sympathetic stimuli → vasoconstriction of digital arteries, dysesthesias
- Botox injection decreases digital pain & improves perfusion
  - Mechanism: inhibits presynaptic release of acetylcholine
- Fails nonoperative treatment: periarterial sympathectomy +/- microvascular reconstruction
- Buerger's disease (thromboangiitis obliterans): vasculitis in smokers → digital ischemia & ulceration due to thrombosis
  - Smoking cessation can reverse disease & prevent amputation

3.5 DEGENERATIVE CONDITIONS

3.5.1 Dupuytren's disease
- Most common in RF, SF
- Contractures due to *myofibroblast* activity: PIP contracture (spiral cord), MCP contracture (central cord), web space contracture (natatory cord), DIP contracture (retrovascular cord)
- Salvage for chronic PIP contracture (attenuation at CS): fusion w/ bone shortening
  - Displaces NV bundle central & superficial
- Cleland's ligament is not involved (dorsal to neurovascular bundle)

- o Think "C for ceiling", Grayson's: "G for ground"—volar to neurovascular bundle
- Treatment: collagenase (most expensive), needle aponeurotomy, fasciectomy
- Most common cause of recurrence: contracture >60°

3.5.2 Ulnocarpal abutment syndrome
- Neutral (normal) ulnar variance: 80% load through radius, 20% through ulna
  - o Positive ulnar variance: greater load through ulna (increases up to 40%) →abutment between ulnar & lunate.
  - o Increases w/ closed fist grip & wrist pronation
- After failing nonoperative treatment, if there is no DRUJ arthritis: ulnar shortening osteotomy
- If there is DRUJ arthritis:
  - o Low-demand patient: Darrach (ulnar head resection)
  - o Manual laborer, high-demand patient: Sauve-Kapandji or ulnar hemiresection arthroplasty with TFCC repair/reconstruction

3.5.3 Basilar thumb arthritis
- 1st web space adduction contracture, MCP hyperextension (Z deformity)—need to address this because leads to adduction contracture which causes basilar joint collapse—failure to address will result in failure of CMC arthroplasty
  - o Treat Z-deformity w/ revision reconstruction w/ APL & MP fusion
- *Trapeziectomy* (most important) with ligament reconstruction & tendon interposition with FCR.
  - o FCR reconstructs 1st intermetacarpal ligament
  - o If FCR is compromised, perform suspension arthroplasty with ECRL or APL tendon
  - o Have to address scaphotrapezotrapezoidal (STT) joint arthritis at time of CMC arthroplasty by excising *proximal trapezoid* (proximal 1/3).

3.5.4 Interphalangeal joint arthritis

- DIP (Heberden's node) vs PIP (Bouchard's node)
- Mucous cyst that has failed nonoperative treatment: mucous cyst excision with osteophyte resection
  - High recurrence if aspiration alone
- Psoriasis: pencil-in-cup deformity, nail pitting (onychodystrophy), skin plaques, dactylitis

3.6 NEUROPATHIES

3.6.1 Brachial plexus injury
- Peripheral nerve inside-out: axon->myelin sheath->endoneurium->fascicles->perineurium->epineurium
  - Order of loss of function (recovery is just the opposite): motor->proprioception->touch->temp->pain->sympathetic
  - Worst recovery after injury: ulnar n & peroneal n
  - Best recovery: radial n
  - Abnormal EMG: sensory latency <3.2m/s, motor latency <4.3m/s; CV <52m/s
- Preganglionic (proximal to DRG)
  - Horner's syndrome (sympathetic chain); medial scapular winging (long thoracic nerve); elevated hemidiaphragm (phrenic nerve); paralysis of rhomboids (dorsal scapular nerve) & cervical paraspinals
  - Preserved sensory nerve action potentials (SNAPs) & therefore normal histamine test
  - CT myelogram is gold standard for diagnosing nerve root injury
- Postganglionic (distal to DRG): abnormal histamine test
  - Better prognosis because of nerve regeneration (1 mm/day)
    - Wallerian degeneration (phagocytosis by macrophages) of distal segment & antegrade regeneration of proximal segment
  - Tinel sign is best predictor of nerve regeneration
- Treatment
  - Oberlin transfer: transfer fascicles of ulnar nerve to motor nerve of biceps
  - Double nerve transfer: transfer (1) fascicles of ulnar nerve to motor nerve of biceps & (2) fascicles of median nerve to motor

nerve of brachialis

3.6.2 Median nerve compression
- Carpal tunnel syndrome
  - Arthroscopic release w/ faster return to work but increased risk of incomplete release
  - Most radial tendon in carpal tunnel: FPL
- AIN: no pain (compared to Parsonage-Turner syndrome) or sensory deficits (motor only)
  - Motor: FPL, FDP of index & long fingers, pronator quadratus
  - Compression sites: ulnar head of pronator teres, FDS arcade
- Pronator syndrome: 5 sites (supracondylar process, ligament of Struthers, bicipital aponeurosis or lacertus fibrosus, FDS aponeurotic arch, between ulnar & humeral heads of pronator teres)
  - Unlike CTS, palmar cutaneous branch of median nerve (innervating palm of hand) is affected in pronator syndrome.
  - Median nerve is b/w ulnar & humeral heads of PT at antecubit; radial a. b/w PT & BR
- Fails nonoperative (including splint) → surgical decompression.

3.6.3 Carpal tunnel syndrome
- Poor prognosis correlates with severity of EMG/NCV studies
  - If there is abnormal EMG/NCV or weak APB, surgery is recommended
- Motor recurrent branch: most common branches after exits tunnel, 30% within, then through
  - Innervation: OP, APB
- Carpal tunnel: FCR is just radial to median nerve; FDS of long & ring fingers are volar (superficial) to FDS of index & small fingers
- Carpal tunnel release: risk for injury to recurrent motor branch of median nerve → APB weakness; minimize by releasing on ulnar side of tunnel
- Grip strength returns to preoperative strength at 12 weeks postoperative.
- Compared to non-op of electrodiagnostic confirmed mild-moderate CTS, surgical treatment w/ *less presence of paresthesias* at 1 year & *improved grip strength*
- CTS with significant thenar wasting: transfer EIP around ulnar wrist

(opponensplasty) to improve opposition function
- Appropriate # opioid pills following CTR: 10

3.6.4 Ulnar nerve compression
- Cubital tunnel syndrome
    - Lowest pressure in cubital tunnel between 30-70° flexion.
    - Test CV across elbow: normal is 50m/s absolute, change <10m/s
    - Risk factor for failure after in-situ decompression & likely need for transposition: *prior trauma* & *younger age*
    - Symptoms are due to vascular obstruction of intraneural vessels
    - Compression sites: between two heads of FCU; arcade of Struthers; Osborne's ligament & MCL; anconeus epitrochlearis.
        - Usually w/ multiple branches to FCU, can sacrifice one prn
    - Froment sign: thumb IP flexion (FPL) compensates for weak adductor pollicis during pinch
    - Wartenberg sign due to weak intrinsics (specifically 3rd palmar interosseous muscle) & unopposed pull of ulnar insertion of extensor digiti minimi (radially innervated).
        - If persistent despite decompression: EDM transfer
    - Crosses IMS 8cm prox to medial epicondyle
    - First dorsal web space atrophy (dorsal interossei)
    - Dorsal sensory branch ulnar nerve (DBUN) leaves 5cm proximal to wrist crease
    - Fails nonoperative (including elbow extension splint) → ulnar nerve decompression (transpose only if there is ulnar nerve subluxation)
- Ulnar tunnel syndrome: most often due to ganglion cyst in Guyon's canal
    - 3 zones of ulnar nerve in tunnel (prox->distal): mixed->motor->sensory
    - Similar symptomatology as cubital tunnel syndrome except: no sensory deficit to dorsum of hand (dorsal cutaneous branch of ulnar nerve); no FCU/FDP weakness
    - Ganglion cyst: mucin-filled, transillumination, perform Allen's test prior to surgery
        - Asymptomatic → observation; symptomatic →

resection

3.6.5 Radial nerve compression
- Radial tunnel syndrome
  - PIN compression with pain but no sensorimotor deficits: pain with resisted long finger extension & forearm supination (can mimic lateral epicondylitis)
    - Pain at 3-4cm distal to lateral epicondyle over mobile wad (vs lateral epicondylitis)
      - Lidocaine diagnostic injection test
    - If there are sensorimotor deficits, it is called PIN compression syndrome
  - Sites of compression: *arcade of Frohse*, leash of Henry, ECRB, fibrous bands anterior to radiocapitellar joint
- Wartenberg's syndrome: compression of superficial sensory radial nerve between BR & ECRL with forearm pronation
- Radial nerve palsy transfer (think someone who wants to still throw football—needs ulnar deviation power)
  - PT to ECRB (for central line of pull wrist-extension)
  - FCR (preserve FCU) to EDC
  - PL to EPL

3.7 CONGENITAL

3.7.1 Radioulnar synostosis
- Failure of segmentation (segmentation occurs from distal to proximal)
- Forearm is often fixed in pronation; shoulder abducts to compensate for lack of pronation
- Consider surgery if functional impairment or bilateral involvement: excision of synostosis with *vascularized* fat patch interposition or forearm derotational osteotomy

3.7.2 Congenital radial head dislocation
- Compared to traumatic dislocation, radial head is convex & capitellum is hypoplastic
  - Bilateral involvement is common; radial head is usually dislocated posteriorly

- Think OI, Larsen's, Achondroplasia
- Usually painless; symptoms at wrist are due to ulnar impaction syndrome
  - o If symptomatic (pain & limited ROM), consider radial head resection after skeletal maturity

3.7.3 Madelung's deformity
- Dyschondrosis of volar & ulnar aspects of distal radial physis → increased volar tilt & radial inclination.
- Abnormal SRL
- Leri-Weill dyschondrosteosis: SHOX mutation; *bilateral* Madelung's deformity; XLD

3.7.4 Radial clubhand (longitudinal radial deficiency)
- Due to defect of apical ectodermal ridge (AER)

Cause	Findings
Thrombocytopenia absent radius (TAR)	Thumb is present
Holt Oram syndrome	Cardiac anomaly
Fanconi anemia	Aplastic pancytopenia, chromosomal breakage test
VATER/VACTERL	

- Workup of longitudinal radial deficiency includes renal US, echo, CBC
- If active elbow flexion (intact biceps function) → ulna centralization & tendon transfers to balance carpus on ulna at 6-12 months of age
- Thumb hypoplasia: CMC stability determines thumb reconstruction with opponensplasty (stable CMC) vs ablation & pollicization (unstable CMC).

3.7.5 Polydactyly
- Preaxial (thumb duplication): Caucasian
  - o Reconstruction: resect smaller thumb (usually radial thumb)
    - ▪ Preserve intrinsic tendon & collateral ligament insertions
- Postaxial (adjacent to small finger): African American (autosomal inheritance: AD)
  - o Postaxial polydactyly in Caucasian requires genetic workup

3.7.6 Camptodactyly
- PIP flexion deformity of small finger → progressive stretching & splinting program
- Camptodactyly-arthropathy-coxa vara-pericarditis syndrome (CACP)

3.7.7 Syndactyly
- Failure of apoptosis of digital web space
- Poland syndrome: unilateral chest wall hypoplasia (absence of sternal head of pectoralis major), unilateral hypoplasia of upper extremity, symbrachydactyly (absent or shortened middle phalanges), simple complete syndactyly.
  - Associated with subclavian artery hypoplasia
- Apert syndrome: FGFR2 mutation
  - Severe, bilateral complex syndactyly (specifically index, long & ring fingers)—"rosebud hands"
  - Intelligence normal to decreased
  - Craniofacial synostosis, symphalangism (fused IP joints); also deformities of feet.
- Syndactyly release & reconstruction usually performed at 1 year of age
  - Web creep is most common complication: web space (commissure) becomes more distal with digital growth

3.7.8 Macrodactyly
- Enlarged phalanges
- Epiphysiodesis: perform when involved digit reaches normal adult length

3.7.9 Amniotic band syndrome
- Also known as Streeter's dysplasia or constrictive ring syndrome
- Swelling distally is due to lymphedema
  - Excise constriction band & perform Z-plasty

3.7.10 Keinbock's disease
- AVN of lunate
  - Risk factors: negative ulnar variance causing increased contact stress between lunate & radius

- CT wrist is best at identifying lunate collapse
- Pediatric: temporary STT pinning
- Adult with pre-collapse or early collapse
  - Negative ulnar variance: radial shortening osteotomy
  - Normal ulnar variance: distal radius core decompression (thought to activate healing/revascular response in lunate)
- Adult with advanced collapse / arthritis: PRC, limited or total wrist arthrodesis, total wrist arthroplasty

3.7.11 Kirner deformity
- Non-syndromic, bilateral, painless
- Thought secondary to abnormal FDP insertion, "z-physis", or AVN
- Radial and volar curve of SF P3

3.8 REPLANTATION

3.8.1 Digital replantation
- Indications
  - Multiple digit amputations
  - Amputation distal to FDS insertion
  - Thumb amputation
  - Amputation in pediatric patient
- Contraindications
  - Ribbon sign
  - Hand (proximal to carpals): warm ischemia time >6h, cold ischemia time >12h; distal to carpals (digits): warm ischemia >12h, cold ischemia >24h
- Indications for revision amp: degloving (need to repair at least 2 veins), bone injury w/ neurovascular damage, injury proximal to FDS insertion/PIP.
- IF ray resection vs MCP-level amp: revision amp w/ wider 1st webspace & thus avoids prominent 1st MC head impingement & improve dexterity; revision amp w/ higher satisfaction scores
  - Some thought that preservation of palmar width with MCP-level amp improves grip strength & thus should be done for heavy laborers
- Order of structures for replantation (BEFANV): bones, extensors,

flexors, arteries, nerves, veins
- o Replant structure-by-structure rather than digit-by-digit
- Arterial thrombosis (within first 12 hrs): remove bandage, place hand in dependent position, heparin, stellate ganglion block
- Venous thrombosis (after first 12 hrs): elevate hand, leech
  - o Leech therapy: risk for Aeromonas infection
    - ▪ Prophylaxis with Cipro or TMP-SMX (if CKD or fluoroquinolone-resistance)
- Reperfusion injury: allopurinol inhibits xanthine oxidase → decrease xanthine, thought to be responsible for reperfusion injury

3.8.2 Soft tissue coverage
- Fingertip injury
  - o Adult with no exposed bone: soft dressing
  - o Pediatric with exposed bone: soft dressing

Flap	Indications
VY advancement flap	Transverse or dorsal oblique fingertip injury
Thenar flap	Volar fingertip injury (overlying P3) to index or long finger • Risk of flexion (PIP) contracture
Cross finger flap	Volar injury to digit (overlying P1/P2)
Reverse cross finger flap	Dorsal injury to digit (overlying P1/P2)
Moberg volar advancement	Volar thumb injury <2cm; most common complication is flexion contracture—better tolerated in thumb than fingers. Moberg requires independent dorsal blood supply—common in thumb, not in fingers
First dorsal metacarpal artery (FDMA) flap	Volar thumb injury >2cm or dorsal thumb injury

- Groin flap: LFCN pierces under inguinal ligament
- Z-plasty lengthening for contracture
  - o 45° limbs → length increases by 50%
  - o 60° limbs → length increases by 75%

3.8.3 Nerve injury & repair

- After peripheral nerve injury, sympathetic activity is last to be lost & first to recover
  - o Motor function is first to be lost & last to return
- 3cm is maximum gap that can be bridged by nerve collagen conduit (use if can't do tensionless repair)
  - o Made of *Type 1 collagen* (this and Type 3 collagen most abundant in peripheral nerves)
  - o Myelin protein zero also commonly found in myelin sheath of peripheral n but not used in nerve conduits
- Radial: best recovery; ulnar/peroneal: worst recovery
- Median nerve lac may require opponensplasty b/c motor is less predictable recovery than sensory
- Motor, sensory ≥3cm, mixed → indications for nerve autograft

3.8.4 Miscellaneous

- Nail bed injury: Dermabond (2-octylcyanoacrylate) is equivalent to suture repair
- Melanonychia striata: brown streaking of nailbed
  - o Often benign, but can be due to a subungual melanoma, which is a rare malignancy
  - o Diagnosis is often delayed, resulting in a higher staging & poorer prognosis
    - ▪ Low threshold for biopsy
- High-pressure injection injury requires I&D in OR.
  - o Factors affecting outcomes: 1) involvement of tendon sheaths, 2) pressure setting, 3) extent of proximal spread, 4) delay to debridement, 5) substance (see below)
    - ▪ Oil-based paints are the worst (highly inflammatory, often need amp) > grease and CFCs (intermediate damage but can debride reasonably) > water (least destructive)
- Hemorrhagic blister: drain blister but leave overlying skin intact
- Can cut A4 and vent A2 as needed if persistent triggering
- Avoid cutting oblique pulley w/ trigger thumb release → bowstringing
- Amputation through proximal phalanx of central digits (RF, LF): stump

gets in the way and also weakens grip → do ray resection
- Wrist scope:
  - 1-2 portal: superficial radial n at risk
  - 6U portal: 4.3mm from DBUN
  - 6R: 8mm from DBUN
- Dorsal compartments radial->ulnar: 1st dorsal compartment (APL—volar in compartment, EPB), 2nd dorsal compartment (ECRL, ECRB), 3rd dorsal compartment (EPL); Listers tubercle; 4th dorsal compartment (EIP, EDC, PIN), 5th dorsal compartment (EDM), 6th dorsal compartment (ECU)
  - 2 dives under 1 at level of wrist
  - Pathology
    - 1st DC: De Quervain's
    - 2nd DC: Intersection syndrome
    - 3rd DC: Drummer's wrist, traumatic rupture w/ DRFx
    - 4th DC: Extensor tenosynovitis
    - 5th DC: Vaughn-Jackson (rupture in RA)
    - 6th DC: Snapping ECU
- Frostbite injury: delay debridement / amputation until necrotic tissue demarcation

3.9 HAND INFECTION

3.9.1 Pyogenic flexor tenosynovitis
- S. aureus is most common
- Animal bite: Pasteurella multocida → gram negative coverage such as ampicillin/sulbactam
- Kanavel's cardinal signs: digit held in flexion, tenderness along tendon sheath, pain with passive extension of digit, fusiform digital swelling
- I&D followed by IV antibiotics

3.9.2 Other deep space infections
- Parona's space: connection between thumb & SF flexor sheaths; between PA & FDP conjoined tendon sheaths
- Thenar (bursa between adductor pollicis & flexor tensons)
- Hypothenar

- Midpalmar

3.9.3 Collar button abscess
- Abscess in web space between fingers
- Need volar & dorsal incisions for thorough I&D

3.10 MISCELLANEOUS

- Pedi phalangeal neck fx or subchondral fx are usually displaced and unstable → CRPP vs ORIF
- MCP dislocation: flex wrist and digits to assist reduction maneuver
- UCL of thumb MP and RCL of IF most important for pinch
- Proximal phalanx fx: transverse, mid-shaft/diaphyseal fx can almost always be treated closed
    - Long/oblique/spiral fx: fix because prone to crossover deformity w/ gripping
- FDS 3&4 are superficial to 2&5 within carpal tunnel
- 25% general population without FDS to small finger
- Proximal carpal row flexes w/ radial deviation and extends with ulnar deviation
- Cleft (split) hand [and foot] deformities are rare congenital conditions common in genetically isolated communities (e.g. Amish). Cosmetically undesirable but otherwise good function if can achieve prehensile grasp.
    - Usually *Autosomal dominant* inheritance; 70% penetrance
- Scaphoid flexes w/ wrist flexion and radial deviation, extends w/ wrist extension and ulnar deviation
- High pressure injection injuries: pressures as low as 100 psi are capable of penetrating the skin. Industrial water jet devices commonly operate between 8,000 and 12,000 psi
- Clenched fist syndrome: factitious disorder w/ crossover deformities and/or flexion contractures of hand w/out organic etiology
    - Usually after minor trauma or surgery
    - Fingers flexed regardless of wrist position
    - Treatment: aggressive therapy + psychiatric support

DOMAIN 4: SPORTS MEDICINE

4.1 BASICS

4.1.1 Anatomy

	Exam tests & signs	Innervation
Subscapularis	Belly press (upper SS), lift off (lower SS), internal rotation lag sign	Upper & lower subscapular nerves (posterior cord)
Supraspinatus	Jobe test, drop arm test	Suprascapular nerve (upper trunk)
Infraspinatus	External rotation lag sign • ER in adduction	Suprascapular nerve (upper trunk)
Teres minor	Hornblower sign • ER in abduction	Axillary nerve (posterior cord)
Teres major	Adducts & internally rotates arm	Lower subscapular nerve (posterior cord)
Biceps tendon	Speed test	
SLAP tear	Obrien test	

- Axillary nerve: anterior branch (deltoid) & posterior branch (teres minor)

4.1.2 Throwing mechanics
- 5 phases: wind up, cocking (early & late), acceleration, deceleration, follow-through
  - Late cocking: maximal ER of shoulder → glenohumeral internal rotation deficit (GIRD) & internal impingement.
    - Period of maximal valgus load at elbow
    - Maximal activation of supraspinatus, infraspinatus, teres minor
  - Acceleration: early muscle activation at triceps; late muscle activation at pecM, latissimus, serratus anterior
  - Deceleration: highest risk to tensile failure of rotator cuff (rotator cuff tear) due to eccentric contraction of rotator cuff to decelerate arm.

- ▪ Highest torque and thus phase most prone to injuries: SLAP, biceps/brachialis/teres minor injuries
  - o Scapula mUst rotate to prevent GT impingement on acromion during *late cocking and acceleration* phases

4.1.3 Concussion
- If diagnosed, can return to play 6 days after injury (there are 6 rehabilitation stages) through a stepwise rehabilitation protocol
- Immediate Post-Concussion Assessment and Cognitive Testing Battery (ImPACT): evaluate athlete's attention, memory & processing speed
- Second-impact syndrome: second traumatic head injury while still recovering from initial injury
  - o Due to disruption of cerebral autoregulation → cerebral vascular congestion, edema & death

4.1.4 Burners & stingers (transient brachial plexus neuropraxia)
- By definition, *unilateral upper extremity* symptoms (pain, paresthesias, sensorimotor deficits)
  - o Return to play when asymptomatic with painless neck ROM

4.1.5 Miscellaneous
- Posterior shoulder (Judet) approach: plane between infraspinatus (suprascapular nerve) & teres minor (axillary nerve)
- Athletic pubalgia (sports hernia): repetitive thigh extension & abduction → strain of adductors (specifically adductor longus).
  - o Aponeurosis between rectus abdominis and adductor longus
- Osteitis pubis: repetitive trauma → pain & osteolysis/erosion of pubic symphysis
- After LHB tenodesis and rehab, no change in shoulder or elbow strength, but need to avoid active supination w/ elbow flexed to 90
  - o Isolated tenotomy associated w/ arm cramping compared to tenodesis
- Piriformis syndrome: compression of sciatic nerve (usually runs *anterior* to piriformis & *posterior* to remaining short external rotators)
- Quadriceps contusion: immobilization with knee flexion for first 24 hours, then physical therapy.

- o Increased risk of myositis ossificans with any deep muscle contusion +/- hematoma formation
- Type III AC injuries (CC and AC ligaments out) treated non-op w/ higher DASH at 6wks/3months and equal function at 1 year compared to operative; lower rate of secondary procedure.
- Modified Weaver-Dunn for CC ligament reconstruction: CA ligament has 20% strength as native CC. Free tendon graft more closely approximates strength of native CC ligament.
- No difference between open and arthroscopic DCE except ability to also evaluate GH joint w/ scope.
- Heat stroke (vs exhaustion): CNS dysfunction
  - o Primary mechanism of heat transfer from skin to environment: evaporation of sweat
  - o Treatment: rapid cooling through immersion in cold or ice water
- Steroids: increase LDL, decrease HDL
- Mononucleosis: EBV infection, splenomegaly; no return to play until 3 weeks after athlete is asymptomatic due to risk of splenic rupture
- Os acromiale: usually between meso- & meta-acromion (Meta-Meso-Pre).
- Calcific tendonitis (dark on MR T1 & T2): diabetes; supraspinatus tendon; deposition of calcium hydroxyapatite. *Resorptive* phase most painful (secondary to phagocytic cells), needling done during this stage.
- Outcomes following scapulothoracic dissociation are dependent upon degree of neuro injury.
  - o Injury is most often associated w/ mortality

4.2 SHOULDER

4.2.1 Rotator cuff tear
- Near end of spectrum of disease from 1) impingement/bursitis (*MMPs* shown to be active during this phase) → 2)partial to full-thickness RCTs → 3) massive RCTs → 4) rotator cuff arthropathy
- Development of symptoms in previously asymptomatic elderly patients is associated with *increase in tear size*
- Subacromial PRP with *no effect on pain, ROM, or function at 1 year compared to PT alone* for subacromial impingement/bursitis

- o Operative management (subacromial decompression) shows lowest outcomes with *workers compensation* claims
- Normal acromiohumeral distance: 7-8mm; normal coracoclavicular distance: 11-13mm
- Supraspinatus tendon footprint: 24mm A-P, 12mm M-L; starts 1.7mm from articular margin of humeral head
  - o Best bone for suture anchor fixation is 1cm lateral/distal to edge of footprint
- Most RCTs articular-sided because it has half strength of bursal side
- ~55% of asymptomatic patients >60yo will have partial and/or full-thickness RCTs on MRI
- If chronic RC issues and acute-onset inability to elevate arm can trial lido injection test: if improved (likely pain-limited) can do supine strengthening program. If not improved (pseudoparalysis), can counsel on rTSA
- PS RCT results in superior HH migration, decreased AH distance
- Rotator cuff functions to compress humeral head against glenoid (dynamic stabilizer of GH joint).
- Lease amount of RC activation in rehab w/ PROM (especially passive FF)
- Degenerative RC tear: initial tear location is 15mm posterior to biceps tendon near supraspinatus/infraspinatus junction.
  - o Trend is people continue to develop new tears and increased pain
- MRA: contrast communicating between glenohumeral joint & subacromial space is diagnostic of RC tear
- Bursal-sided RC tear >3mm (25% thickness) or articular-sided RC tear >6mm (50% thickness) in depth: convert to full thickness tear & perform rotator cuff repair.
  - o Partial articular sided tears <50%: debride
    - ▪ Note: *7mm* exposed bony footprint b/w tuberosity and intact tendon indicates >50% thickness
- Subscapularis tear will lead to subluxation of biceps tendon medially.
  - o Is an absolute contraindication to SCR
  - o Arthroscopic subscapularis repair: SGHL/CHL are landmarks for upper border repair—"comma sign".

76

- CHL is extension of rotator cable at avascular zone
  - o Irreparable subscapularis tear: pectoralis major transfer (puts musculocutaneous nerve at risk).
    - To reduce risk of neuropraxia, PM transfer is under conjoint but superficial to MSCT nerve (lateral cord)
    - Note: for LD transfer you need intact subscap!
- During arthroscopy, to better visualize SS tendon insertion on LT do the *posterior lever push*—IR + posterior stress on humeral head
- Teres minor insufficiency: positive Hornblowers signs (arm abducted 90deg and inability to ER)
- Calculating partial-thickness RC tear: supraspinatus tendon medial-lateral width is normally between 12.1 to 12.7mm
- Double-row repair: lower retear rate than single-row repair (more anatomic).
- After rotator cuff repair, there is no difference in outcomes between early & delayed physical therapy.
- Tendon to bone healing w/ RCTs takes 8-12 weeks
  - o Bone anchor drilling and peribursal tissue are source of vascularity for healing. Can also increase vascularity w/ exercise (gentle)
  - o Need to protect repair for 6-8 weeks (PROM only), but do need some physiologic tension with immobilization because no tension decreases cross-sectional area of repair site
- MCC of failure is failure of cuff to heal 2/2 *suture pull out from repair site*.
  - o Goutallier grade (fatty infiltration), age, initial tear size, and concomitant biceps/AC procedures are greatest *risk factors* for nonhealing after repair
- Irreparable subscapularis tear (internal rotation deficiency): pectoralis major transfer
  - o Musculocutaneous nerve at risk during harvest of PM
- Irreparable supraspinatus/infraspinatus tear
  - o Young, laborer: latissimus dorsi transfer
    - Radial nerve is at risk during harvest of LD
  - o Elder: rTSA
- Interscalene regional block: risk for tension pneumothorax (Beck's triad: distended neck veins, distant heart sounds, hypotension)

- o Emergent needle decompression/thoracostomy in 2nd intercostal space
- Lateral decubitus position decreases concern for cerebral hypoperfusion (vs beach-chair)
- Inferior placement of posterior shoulder portal puts *axillary* nerve at risk for injury
- After shoulder arthroscopy, intraarticular bupivacaine pump increases risk for *chondrolysis*.
- 65-75% increased rate of post-op infection in patients w/in *1 month* of receiving corticosteroid injection. Returns to baseline after 3 months.

4.2.2 Rotator cuff arthropathy
- Pseudoparalysis with anterosuperior escape of humeral head
    - o Anterosuperior humeral head migration occurs when both rotator cuff & coracoacromial ligament are deficient
- Young, active: hemiarthroplasty
- SCR shown to have good outcomes if massive irreparable SS/IS tears *without superior migration of HH on XR*
- Elder: rTSA; requires intact deltoid function
    - o Concomitant external rotation deficiency: LD transfer
        - Worse outcomes after LD transfer if fatty atrophy of supra/IS, deltoid weakness, subscap deficiency, or non-synergistic action of LD. CA ligament absence has no effect on outcome.
        - Revision surgery is RF for complication (37% revision, 13% w/ primary)
        - Associated w/ infection in rTSA: younger age, male gender
    - o Inferior scapular notching: medial aspect of humeral cup impinges on lateral scapula during adduction
        - Risk factors: superior placement of baseplate & superior tilt of baseplate
            - Inferior placement of baseplate is most important in decreasing rate of scapular notching

4.2.3 SLAP tear

- Associated with GIRD & spinoglenoid cyst
- Arthroscopic repair: suprascapular nerve is at risk (especially when there is medial perforation of glenoid neck)
  - Suprascapular nerve arises from superior trunk
- If patient is older and/or there is associated degenerative fraying of biceps or instability →biceps tenodesis
  - Tenodesis techniques have equivalent functional outcomes (supra vs subpectoral tenodesis)

4.2.4 Glenohumeral internal rotation deficit (GIRD)
- Sleeper stretch to address posteroinferior capsule tightness
- Internal impingement: articular-sided (undersurface) rotator cuff pathology
  - Late cocking/early acceleration of throwing: maximum shoulder abduction & ER → impingement of supraspinatus tendon against *posterosuperior* glenoid
    - Can cause partial articular sided supraspinatus tendon avulsion (PASTA)
    - Maximum shoulder ABD & ER causes significant tension of posteroinferior capsule → mineralization/exostosis of posteroinferior glenoid & posterior band of IGHL (traction spur, or Bennett lesion)
    - Shoulder ABD & ER (apprehension test) will produce pain
  - GIRD shoulder: humeral head shifts posterosuperior during late cocking/early acceleration.

4.2.5 Biceps tendonitis
- Long head of biceps predominantly attaches on *posterior* aspect of glenoid
  - *Proximal* biceps tendon rupture results in Popeye deformity
- After long head of biceps tenodesis, avoid seated active forearm supination with elbow flexed to 90°, but after formal rehab there is no change in shoulder or elbow strength.
- Tenotomy: more arm cramping & Popeye deformity; no difference in strength between tenotomy & tenodesis.

4.2.6 Little leaguer's shoulder
- Proximal humerus Salter Harris I physeal injury (hypertrophic zone)
    o Xrays: widened physis
- Stop pitching, PT → progressive throwing program

4.2.7 Adhesive capsulitis
- Contracture of rotator interval & coracohumeral ligament (CHL) → decreased intracapsular volume, loss of axillary recess
- Release of rotator interval (anterior-superior capsule) will increase ER with arm by side (most limited ROM); release of posterior capsule will increase IR
- Fibroblastic proliferation on histology
- Diabetes is a poor prognostic factor; also associated with hypothyroidism
    o Initial workup includes HbA1c & TSH levels

4.2.8 Scapular winging
- Medial: long thoracic nerve (C5, C6, C7) → serratus anterior
- Lateral: CN11 (spinal accessory nerve) → trapezius.
    o Dorsal scapular n → rhomboids
- Initial treatment is nonoperative (physical therapy & activity modification).

4.2.9 Distal clavicle osteolysis
- Weightlifters & laborers: stress reaction in distal clavicle from repetitive trauma → hyperemic response, localized bone resorption, cyst formation
- Refractory to nonoperative treatment: distal clavicle resection
- When doing distal clavicle excision (DCE), need to keep <1cm

4.2.10 Suprascapular neuropathy
- Suprascapular notch: supraspinatus, infraspinatus
    o Suprascapular artery runs above suprascapular ligament; suprascapular nerve runs below

- Spinoglenoid notch: infraspinatus

4.2.11 Pectoralis major rupture
- Tendinous avulsion off bone during *eccentric* contraction (e.g., downward deceleration during bench press)
- Pectoralis major inserts on humeral shaft lateral to bicipital groove → adduction & IR of arm
- Innervated by medial & lateral pectoral nerves.

4.2.12 Quadrilateral space syndrome
- Contents: PHCA & axillary nerve
- Borders: LH triceps (medial), Tminor (superior), Tmajor (inferior), Humerus (lateral)

4.3 ELBOW

4.3.1 Distal biceps tendon rupture
- Obtain MRI with elbow flexed, shoulder abducted & forearm supinated to increase study sensitivity
    - Forearm supination with elbow flexed is mediated by biceps
- Within antecubital fossa, biceps tendon travels lateral (radial) to median nerve & posterior (deep) to recurrent radial artery
- Partial tear (positive Hook test) usually occurs on radial side of bicipital tuberosity
    - Fails nonoperative treatment: complete tear & repair
- Complete rupture: loss of supination strength greater than flexion strength
    - Recommend acute surgical repair
    - Nonoperative treatment will lead to 40% loss of supination & 30% loss of elbow flexion strength
- Single incision: LABCN injury (branch of MC nerve)—most common complication following repair (single or dual incision; 13-21%); can also injure radial nerve/PIN/superficial sensory radial nerve.
- Dual incision: heterotopic ossification; more anatomic placement of biceps repair
- *LABCN neuropraxia* is most common complication following repair

81

(rate of 13-21%); less common: re-rupture (1.4-1.8%), PIN palsy (1.3-1.9%), HO (0.5-3.6%)
- If can't reapproximate w/ ≤ 90° flexion → allograft
    o However, if need to hyperflex for fixation, NO loss of ROM or resultant flexion contracture

4.3.2 Little leaguer's elbow
- Medial elbow pain secondary to UCL injury, medial epicondyle stress fracture or strain of flexor-pronator muscle group
    o Xrays: widening of medial epicondylar apophysis
- Pitcher: most valgus stress on elbow during late cocking/early *Acceleration* (associated w/ maximal glenohumeral ER)
    o Avoid pitching for at least 4 months out of the year
    o Glenohumeral IR is most protective to valgus load at elbow
- Little league pitcher can also develop olecranon stress fracture: posteromedial elbow pain, widening of olecranon apophysis
    o If fails nonoperative treatment → ORIF with compression screw

4.3.3 Pitcher's elbow (valgus extension overload)
- Osteophytes develop in posteromedial tip of olecranon
    o Pain usually in deceleration phase
    o Fails nonoperative treatment → arthroscopic excision
        ▪ Most common reason for repeat surgery is valgus instability (avoid over-resection of olecranon)
- MUCL anatomy
    o MCL itself provides >50% valgus stability in 90° flexion, 30% in full extension (radial head is primary in extension)
    o Anterior oblique bundle: primary stabilizer to valgus stress (moving valgus stress test); strongest (260N)
        ▪ Anterior band: tight in extension (0-90°); *isometric* strain pattern through elbow ROM
        ▪ Posterior band: tight in flexion (90-120°)
    o Posterior oblique bundle: greatest change in tension from flexion (tight) to extension
    o Transverse band.
- UCL *reconstruction* (not repair) typically with palmaris longus

autograft
- o Graft covers posterior 25% of radial head and tightened in 45° flexion and neutral rotation
- o Most common complication is ulnar neuritis
- o Docking technique provides higher rate of return to play & lower complication rate compared to Jobe & modified Jobe techniques

4.3.4 Posterolateral rotatory instability of elbow
- LUCL injury from elbow dislocation or iatrogenic during debridement of lateral epicondylitis
  - o Lateral elbow dissection / debridement anterior to equator of capitellum/radial head to avoid injury to LUCL
- Lateral pivot shift test: forearm supination & valgus stress while bringing elbow from extension to flexion → extension dislocates & flexion reduces radiocapitellar joint
- Instability with chair rise
- LUCL reconstruction with palmaris longus autograft

4.3.5 Lateral epicondylitis
- Tendinitis at origin of ECRB; ECRB inserts at base of third metacarpal
- Tendon gliding exercises
- Steroid injection does not affect outcomes
- Histology: angiofibroblastic hyperplasia / proliferation
- Fails nonoperative treatment: debridement & release of ECRB

4.3.6 Medial epicondylitis
- Tendinitis at origin of flexor pronator mass
- Most common coexisting pathology is ulnar neuropathy at cubital tunnel
- Histology: angiofibroblastic hyperplasia
- Fails nonoperative treatment: debridement & reattachment of flexor pronator mass

4.4 HIP

4.4.1 Snapping hip (coxa saltans)
- Internal: iliopsoas tendon sliding over iliopectineal eminence or femoral head
  - o Provocative test: reproduce popping when hip is moved from FABER to neutral position
  - o Treatment: cortisone injection, psoas tendon release
    - ▪ During hip arthroscopy, zona orbicularis is landmark for IP tendon
- External: iliotibial band sliding over greater trochanter
  - o Ober test evaluates tightness of TFL/IT band: limited hip adduction when extremity is fully extended

4.4.2 Femoroacetabular impingement (FAI)
- Nonspherical femoral head within hemispheric acetabulum
- Associated hip labral tear is usually *anterosuperior*
- Anterior impingement test (hip flexion, ADD, IR) reproduces pain
  - o Anterior impingement can result in "contra-coup" chondral injury on *posteroinferior acetabulum*
- Cam FAI: athletic male, femoral neck retroversion, alpha angle (>42° is abnormal)
- Pincer FAI (prominent anterosuperior acetabular rim): middle-aged female, acetabular retroversion, crossover sign
- Dunn XR: most sensitive & specific for FAI (CAM)
- False profile XR: best to assess for anterior acetabular bone loss
- Most common reason for revision hip arthroscopy for FAI is persistent impingement (residual cam or pincer deformity)
- If open surgical hip dislocation is required, perform trochanterip flip osteotomy to protect MCFA
  - o After open FAI treatment, adolescent athletes return to sports at 7 months

4.4.3 Hip arthroscopy
- Traction neuropraxia of *pudendal* nerve is most common
- Anterolateral portal: superior gluteal nerve
- Posterolateral portal: sciatic nerve, especially if hip is ER when establishing portal

- Anterior portal: LFCN, femoral NV bundle

4.4.4 Hamstring tear
- Usually tear at *myotendinous junction* during sprinting (during eccentric contraction when hip is flexed & knee extended)
  - Satellite cells are involved in muscle regeneration after injury
- Acute muscle injury: neutrophils are first cells to appear (just like in acute infection)
  - TGF-β stimulates myofibroblast proliferation → increased fibrosis

4.5 KNEE

4.5.1 Osteology
- Lateral femoral condyle is longer in A-P diameter and straighter than MFC (MFC is shorter and more oblique)
  - LFC has face of 10° off sagittal plane ("straighter") compared to MFC which has face of 25° off sagittal plane ("more oblique")
    - Thus, to look down face of either condyle you need to ER 10 degrees for LFC and IR 25 degrees for MFC
- MFC is more posterior and distal. LFC is more anterior and proximal
  - Tibia plateau is in 3 degrees varus from shaft, thus MFC needs to be more distal in extension and more posterior in flexion
- Lateral plateau is convex and proximal, medial plateau is concave and distal
  - Medial plateau is larger in A-P dimension
- Past 30 degrees flexion, primary restraint to lateral patellar subluxation is LFC (bony anatomy)
  - 0-20°: MPFL
    - MPFL inserts just proximal to sMCL, anterior and distal to adductor tubercle to superomedial border of patella at junction of proximal and medial 1/3s

4.5.2 Discoid meniscus
- 3-5% general population, ¼ bilateral of those with discoid
- Lateral meniscus more common than medial meniscus, bilateral in 20%

of cases
  - o   Xrays: squaring of lateral femoral condyle, cupping of lateral tibia plateau
- Diagnosis: presence of meniscus on ≥3 consecutive sagittal MRI images ("bow-tie sign")
- Wrisberg variant (type 3): lacks posterior meniscotibial attachments, treat w/ repair & creation of posterior meniscotibial attachments
- Failed conservative treatment: arthroscopic saucerization & repair

4.5.3 Meniscal injury

- Meniscus is fibrocartilaginous: Type 1 collagen
- Standing: withstands 50% of load knee, flexed: 85% load of knee
- Medial: C-shaped, peripheral 20-30% vascularized
- Lateral: more circular, more mobile, peripheral 10-25% vascularized
- Medial meniscus is less mobile (more soft tissue attachments) than lateral meniscus → medial meniscus more prone to injury (especially posterior horn)—3x more common than lateral meniscal tear
  - o   Exception: lateral meniscal injury is more common with acute ACL tear
  - o   Main secondary posterior restraint of femur on tibia is PHMM
- Medial & lateral *inferior genicular arteries* supply periphery of menisci → peripheral tears (red zone) have better healing potential than central tears (white zone; relies on diffusion from joint space)
  - o   Smaller meniscal rim width (distance from tear to periphery/meniscosynovial junction) → better healing potential due to better blood supply
  - o   Ideal tear: <4cm, red zone ("small rim width"), vertical, longitudinal.
- Joint line tenderness is most sensitive exam finding
- Double PCL sign: bucket-handle tear of medial meniscus
- Baker (parameniscal) cyst: between semimembranosus & *medial* head of gastrocnemius
- Strongest predictor of outcome following meniscectomy: degree of osteoarthritis (modified Outerbridge cartilage score) at time of surgery
- Gold standard: inside-out technique with vertical mattress sutures
  - o   Lateral meniscal tear: approach is between posterolateral joint

capsule (posterior to LCL) & lateral head of gastrocnemius
- o Medial meniscal tear: approach is between posteromedial joint capsule (posterior to MCL) & medial head of gastrocnemius
- Absolute contraindication to meniscal transplantation: inflammatory arthritis
- Perimeniscal cysts: radial tears, w/in meniscus
- Parameniscal cysts: more common, complex or longitudinal tears next to/outside meniscus; can lead to Baker's cyst—between medial head of GS and semimembranosus

4.5.4 ACL tear & reconstruction
- ACL dimensions: 33mm x 11mm; native strength of 2200N
- 4.5:1 female-male ratio
  - o Females also at increased of retear following return to sport
- COL5A1 is protective!
- Chronic ACL deficiency → complex medial meniscal tears (PHMM is main secondary posterior restraint of femur on tibia)
- ACL is *extrasynovial*; receives blood supply from *middle geniculate artery* (from popliteal artery)
  - o Lateral & medial inferior/superior genicular arteries supply lateral & medial menisci
- Segond fracture: avulsion of anterolateral ligament
- Injury prevention in female athletes: neuromuscular training / coordination
  - o COL5A1 polymorphism is associated with lower risk for ACL rupture in women
- Reconstruction after physical therapy when motion & gait are normal
- No difference between accelerated vs non-accelerated rehab program after surgery
  - o Avoid open chain exercises (e.g., seated leg extension)
- Bone bruises on MRI is a predictor of motion deficit following ACL reconstruction
  - o Middle $1/3^{rd}$ of *lateral* femoral condyle (sulcus terminalis) & posterior $1/3^{rd}$ of *lateral* tibial plateau
- Under 40 years old: autograft preferred over allograft because of lower

reruperure rate.
- Bone patellar tendon bone (BPTB) autograft has the most tensile stiffness / strength; fastest incorporation
  - 30% rate of knee pain
  - 8-12 weeks: risk of patella tendon rupture
- HS autograft (or quad): 4000-4400N
  - Risk: "windshield wipering" effect
- Hamstring autograft: 8.5mm is smallest diameter that can minimize risk for rupture
- Age >50 and comorbidity scores >5 are associated w/ increased risk of progression to OA requiring TKA
- Bifurcate ridge separates femoral attachment sites of anteromedial & posterolateral bundles.
  - *Posterolateral* bundle is responsible for rotatory stability of knee (pivot shift); anteromedial bundle restrains anterior tibial translation (anterior drawer)
    - Pivot shift test: when knee is extended & internal rotation/valgus force is applied, lateral tibial plateau subluxates anterolaterally; as knee is flexed, lateral plateau slides posteriorly & reduces, producing an audible "clunk"
    - Reconstructed knee has improved pivot shift test postoperatively
- Drilling femoral tunnel via anteromedial portal allows more anatomic graft placement compared to transtibial drilling
- Resident's ridge (lateral intercondylar ridge) is arthroscopic landmark for femoral tunnel drilling in ACL reconstruction—1-2mm from posterior cortex and behind resident's ridge
  - *Anterior* femoral tunnel placement: most common error → loss of knee flexion (graft tight in flexion), stretching (elongation) of graft over time
  - Vertical femoral tunnel → rotational instability (failure to reconstruct posterolateral bundle) & impingement against PCL
- Tibial tunnel: 9mm posterior to posterior aspect of intermeniscal ligament
  - When knee is fully extended, tibial tunnel should lie *behind* a line extending from Blumensaat's line

- o Anterior tibial tunnel: graft tight in flexion & notch impingement with extension
  - o Posterior tibial tunnel: may impinge on PCL
- Most common reason for ACL reconstruction failure is malposition of bone tunnels
- Greatest risk factor for recurrent ACL rupture after reconstruction is patient *age*
- Graft-screw divergence >30° decreases pullout strength → fixation failure
- *S. epidermidis* is most common cause of septic arthritis following ACL reconstruction (*S. aureus* is second)
- Pediatric ACL reconstruction: physeal sparring techniques to (1) prevent tibial recurvatum (tibial tubercle apophyseal arrest) & (2) prevent LLD and/or angular deformity (distal femoral physeal arrest).
- Concomitant injuries:
  - o PLC: do before or at same time of ACLR
  - o MCL: let heal for varus/valgus stability
  - o Meniscus: at or same time because thought that bleeding stimulated healing
  - o Coronal/sagittal malalignment: HTO before or during ACLR
- Complications
  - o During rehab, critical is full extension. If lacks despite PT → MRI to eval for cyclops lesion
  - o S. aureus (most commonly w/in 2 weeks): I&D + 6 weeks IV abx
  - o Arthrofibrosis > 3 weeks: MUA +/- LOA
  - o Saphenous injury: between layers 1&2; minimize w/ knee flexion and hip ER during harvest
    - ▪ Infrapatellar branch of saphenous (innervates med→lat); injury results in inferolateral knee numbness
  - o Infrapatellar contraction syndrome: decreased A/P ROM, patella baja

4.5.5 PCL injury
- Dimensions: 38mm x 13mm
- Resists 2600-3000N posterior-directed force

- Extrasynovial; origin: posterior tibia sulcus; insertion: AL MFC
- Meniscotibial ligaments (Humphrey's—anterior, Wrisberg—posterior):
  - Originate from PHLM and insert onto PCL
- Direct blow (dashboard injury) or fall onto flexed knee with foot in plantarflexion
- Chronic PCL deficiency causes arthritis in *medial & patellofemoral* knee compartments, also w/ varus deformity (need to address w/ HTO before reconstruction)
- Blood supply: middle geniculate artery
- Anterolateral (primary) & posteromedial bundles
  - AL bundle is primary restraint to P force in 90 degrees flexion
    - AL tight in flexion.
- Physical therapy with focus on *quadriceps* strengthening (to counter posterior translation of tibia)
  - Form of *closed chain* strengthening after 10-14 days of protection
- PCL reconstruction: tension graft at 90° of knee flexion (native anterolateral bundle is tight in flexion)
  - PM portal (arthroscopy): risk of injury to *saphenous nerve*
  - Avoid immediate hamstring exercises after reconstruction (hamstring pulls tibia posteriorly & thus stresses the graft)
- PCL injury treatment
  - OR if multilig knee or bony avulsion (ORIF)
    - Scope transtibial w/ PM portal
    - Open tibial inlay: interval b/w SM and medial gastric
      - Also use for ORIF if avulsion
      - Watch out for popliteal artery—screws for open technique are w/in 20mm
    - Post-op: briefly immobilized in extension
  - Isolated G1 or G2 PCL: non-op w/ quad PT, return to play at 2-4 wks
- When performing HTO to correct varus malalignment in a PCL-deficient knee, *increasing* tibial slope will decrease posterior tibial subluxation (increasing slope will cause femur to roll more posterior relative to tibia) → greater stability
  - Similarly, in ACL-deficient knee, decreasing slope will shift tibia posteriorly → less anterior translation of tibia & therefore

knee is more stable
- o Lateral vs medial HTO (to produce valgus and offload medial compartment)
  - ▪ Medial (opening wedge): avoids CPN injury
  - ▪ Lateral (closing wedge): more stable, early weightbearing, avoid patella baja

4.5.6 MCL injury
- Usually ligamentous avulsion at femoral insertion.
- Deep fibers of MCL resist rotatory stress, superficial fibers resist valgus stress
  - o Posterior oblique ligament (POL) stabilizes medial side of knee in extension
- Proximal tears heal better than distal tears; proximal are more common.
- Associated w/ medial meniscus tears due to more capsular attachments (compared to lateral meniscus)
- sMCL & dMCL separated by bursa
  - o sMCL is primary restraint to valgus in 30 deg flexion, PMC is primary restraint in full extension
    - ▪ sMCL is proximal 3mm & posterior 4mm to medial epicondyle and inserts broadly at level of articular surface and 6cm distally where it inserts into periosteum deep to pes
  - o dMCL: capsular thickening, associated w/ medial meniscus via coronary ligaments
    - ▪ Blends posteriorly w/ POL (POL resists IR of tibia in full extension)
- Stener lesion: G3 MCL injury in which distal aspect tears and flips proximally over pes

4.5.7 LCL injury
- Femoral origin of LCL is posterior & proximal relative to insertion of popliteus
  - o POP is DAD: popliteus is distal, anterior & deep
  - o LCL inserts proximal & posterior to lateral femoral epicondyle
- LCL inserts on fibular head *anterior* to popliteofibular ligament

- Posterolateral corner injury
  - Associated w/ MFC and MTP bone bruises
  - PLC is primary stabilizer to tibia ER, but also helps prevent A→P translation of tibia and varus
  - PLC anatomy
    - (1) Biceps femoris: this & ITB make up first layer of knee
      - Posterior to ITB; most posterior insertion on fibular head
      - Short head of biceps is only muscle in thigh innervated by peroneal division of sciatic n
      - CPN lies behind biceps (between layers 1 & 2—layer 2 is patellar retinaculum and PFL)
      - ITB: anterior to biceps; inserts onto Gerdy's; innervated by SGN (TFL) & acts as both extensor and flexor at knee (mechanism behind pivot shift test)
      - Lateral head of GS also acts as dynamic stabilizer of PLC
    - (2) LCL: origin lateral epicondyle, insertion is *most anterior* insertion on fibular head (think "first" collateral ligament)
      - Inserts 1.4mm prox & 3.1mm posterior to lateral epicondyle; proximal and posterior to popliteus
      - Stress in varus and 30 deg flexion
      - Behind COR of knee so tight in extension, lax in flexion
    - (3) Popliteus: origin back of tibia, runs intraarticular through sulcus & inserts at popliteal sulcus 18.5mm anterior and distal to insertion of LCL on lateral epicondyle
      - "POP is MAD"—medial, anterior, distal (to LCL attachment)
    - (4): PFL: origin fibula (posterior to LCL, anterior to biceps), insertion is MT junction of popliteus
    - Structures 2-4 (LCL, popliteus, PFL) make up the 3

"reconstructed" structures in PLC reconstruction and make up layer 3 of knee

- o Reverse pivot shift: valgus + ER in flexion → PL subluxation reduces w/ extension
- o Dial test
  - \> 10° of external rotation at 30° but not at 90° of knee flexion: isolated PLC injury
  - \> 10° of external rotation at 30° & 90° of knee flexion: combined PLC & PCL injuries
- o PLC injury treatment
  - Low-grade sprain: immobilize in extension x 2 weeks f/b PT for quads
  - Avulsion: fix
  - Tear: can try to repair; if unable → allograft recon of PFL and LCL f/b immobilization x 2 weeks f/b ROM at 4 weeks (quads yes, hamstrings no)
- o Other static stabilizing ligaments of lateral knee
  - Arcuate ligament
    - Capsular thickening; "Y"-shaped form lateral epicondyle and inserts on fibula deep to LCL, PFL, biceps
    - "Arcuate sign" is avulsion fx of fibular head
  - Fabellofibular ligament: capsular thickening

4.5.8 Osgood-Schlatter disease

- Fails nonoperative treatment: ossicle resection & tibial tubercleplasty
- Tibial tubercle secondary ossification center forms 11-14yo, fuses b/w 14-18yo
- Traction apophysitis at *inferior pole* of patella is called Sinding- Larsen-Johansson syndrome

4.5.9 Osteochondritis dissecans (OCD) of knee

- Most common in posterolateral aspect of *medial* femoral condyle
- Microfracture: perforates subchondral bones to stimulate mesenchymal stem cells to fill defect with *fibrocartilage* (type I collagen)
- In general:

- o   <2cm by 2cm defect: microfracture or osteochondral autograft (mosaicplasty)
    - ▪   OATS plugs of bone/cartilage from NWB surfaces (ex: femoral trochlea)
- o   >2cm by 2cm defect: osteochondral allograft transplantation (OAT) or autologous chondrocyte implantation (ACI).
    - ▪   OAT: tissue bank live chondrocytes matched by size and shape preop
        - •   Can do big defects but risk of infection
    - ▪   ACI: cartilage harvested and cultured; implanted w/ dermal patch over subchondral bone (2 stages)
        - •   Grows cartilage most like hyaline rather than fibrocartilage
        - •   No size or shape limitations but equivalent outcomes to microfracture
    - ▪   MACI: like ACI but glued into place rather than sewn under patch
        - •   Grows both articular (type 2 collagen) and fibrocartilage (type 1 collagen)
    - ▪   Note: need to consider Marquette or Fulkerson TTO if patellofemoral harvesting
- •   Autologous osteochondral mosaicplasty: bone graft will incorporate into subchondral bone & cartilage will remain viable
- •   Patellofemoral chondral lesions: autologous chondrocyte implantation (ACI) with anteromedial tibial tubercle transfer provides better results than ACI alone
- •   **Pediatric osteochondritis dissecans (OCD)**
    - o   Capitellum & posterolateral MFC most common
        - ▪   Wilson test: pain w/ IR tibia that is relieved w/ ER
    - o   *Stable* lesion in patient with *open* physis: activity modification, bracing, protected weight bearing x 6 months.
        - ▪   Open physis (young patient) is best predictor of success with nonoperative treatment; also those in MFC
            - •   Worse prognosis if LFC lesions, those on patella, *closed physes*, and/or MRI w/ evidence of synovial fluid behind lesion
        - ▪   *Stable* lesion, fails nonoperative treatment: subchondral drilling

- *Unstable* lesion: arthroscopic fixation

4.5.10 Patellar instability

- Risk factors for lateral instability: lateral patellar tilt (tight lateral retinaculum), lateral patellofemoral angle that opens medially, TT- TG distance >20mm, high Q angle, femoral IR (anteversion) or tibial ER (external tibial torsion), patella alta (leads to J-sign), weak VMO compared to vastus lateralis / IT band, female, younger age
- MPFL femoral attachment is between medial epicondyle & adductor tubercle
    o Most common injury is MPFL soft-tissue avulsion off femoral attachment
    o Traumatic lateral patellar dislocation: most common osteochondral injury is medial patellar facet
- First episode of patellar instability without acute chondral injury or loose bodies: nonoperative (brace, PT)
- MPFL reconstruction: femoral insertion is at Schottle point (anterior to line extending distally along posterior cortex of femoral shaft & proximal to Blumensaat's line)
    o Tension MPFL at 30° knee flexion
    o If femoral tunnel too proximal: tight in flexion
    o If femoral tunnel too distal: loose in flexion
- Consider anteromedial tibial tubercle transfer if TT-TG >20mm
    o Lateral patellar instability normally causes increased contact pressure over inferior & lateral aspects of patella
        ▪ Anteromedialization of TT will increase contact pressure over superior & medial aspects of patella

4.5.11 Quadriceps tendon rupture

- Suture anchor fixation results in smaller gap formation & higher ultimate failure strength than transosseous suture fixation

4.5.12 Tibial stress syndrome (shin splints)

- Traction periostitis of posterior tibialis & soleus → *medial* (posteromedial) tibial stress syndrome (more common)
- Traction periostitis of anterior tibilias → anterior (anterolateral) tibial

stress syndrome
- Unlike tibial stress fracture, pain improves with training / running
    o Tibial stress fracture: anterior (tension-side) is more difficult to heal than compression-side

DOMAIN 5: HIP & KNEE

5.1 BASICS

5.1.1 Arthritis
- Rheumatoid arthritis: T-cell mediated autoimmune disease
  - Rheumatoid factor is an IgM autoantibody that targets IgG
  - Best test is anti-CCP (cyclic citrullinated peptide)
  - TNFα inhibitors: infliximab, etanercept, adalimumab
    - Treatment for ankylosing spondylitis, RA
    - Hold 1 week prior to & 2 weeks after surgery
  - Anakinra: IL1 receptor antagonist
  - Rituximab: inhibits CD20 (B cells)
  - Abatacept: fusion protein that inhibits T cells
- Juvenile idiopathic arthritis (JIA, or JRA): <16 years old, elevated ESR / ANA
  - Need ophthalmologic evaluation (slit lamp exam)
  - Like RA, can have atlantoaxial instability
  - Like RA, treat with DMARDs
- Reiter's syndrome: arthritis, urethritis, conjunctivitis/uveitis
- In general, for surgery, can continue MTX, leflunomide, hydroxychloroquine
  - Hold TNF antagonists 1 week before & resume 2 weeks after surgery
  - Surgery 7 months after last rituximab dose
  - For Stelara (biologic agent; ustekinumab), schedule surgery 1 week after last dose & hold for minimum 14 days after surgery as incisions heal

5.1.2 Wear
- Volumetric wear = $\pi \cdot r^2 \cdot w$ where w is linear wear
- PE is best made by *direct-compression molding* of powder to insert (best wear properties)
- Crosslinking PE (UHMWPE) *improves* wear resistance (especially adhesive wear) but *reduces* mechanical properties (e.g., fracture toughness, tensile strength)

        o   Sterilization of PE is done by irradiation in *inert* gas; irradiation generates free radicals which facilitate cross-linking of PE & improve wear; however, too much free radicals (i.e., irradiation in presence of air) is bad because they cause oxidative degradation of PE

- Remelting (heat PE past melting point) & annealing (heat PE close to melting point) remove excess free radicals after irradiation
  - Annealing increases while remelting decreases crystal formation of UHMWPE

- Ceramic-on-ceramic bearing couple provides least volumetric wear (best bearing surfaces)
  - However, it is at risk for catastrophic failure of acetabular liner (fracture of ceramic liner with fragments in joint)
    - Characteristic *stripe wear* pattern from lift-off separation of femoral head coming into contact with acetabular rim
    - Risk factors for stripe wear & thus liner fracture: vertical cup, morbid obesity
  - Squeaking
- Metal-on-metal produces smaller wear particles than metal on PE
  - Metal-on-metal wear particles stimulate *lymphocytes* → pseudotumor (aseptic, lymphocyte-dominated, vasculitis-associated lesion (ALVAL))
  - Cup abduction >55° is associated with elevated serum metal ion levels
- Urinary N-telopeptide (breakdown product of type 1 collagen) is a marker for osteolysis.
- PO and topical TXA universally accepted as beneficial in reducing post-op blood loss following TKA/THA.

5.2 HIP

5.2.1 Avascular necrosis of femoral head
- Best predictor of pain is bone marrow edema on MRI
- Kerboul angle (combined necrotic angle) >240° poses high risk for femoral head collapse
- Bisphosphonates to prevent femoral head collapse

- Sickle cell: natural history of AVN is progressive loss of sphericity of femoral head

5.2.2 Primary total hip replacement

- Per AAOS CPGs, *pharmacologic and mechanical VTE ppx* has highest level of evidence for preventing DVT following THA/TKA
- Anterior approach does not show superior gait mechanics compared to posterior or anterolateral
- Posterior approach with increased hip adduction moment and longer step length
- Monoblock cups have liner embedded w/in acetabular component— need to exchange entire acetabular component if revision indicated.
  - o If revising monoblock cup due to instability, consider constrained liner or dual mobility
- Morse taper construct assembly requires *4000N* of force over a *dry* taper
  - o For femoral stems, early design was 14/16 but currently most surgeons prefer 12/14 taper
  - o Factors that increase risk of corrosion: wet taper, taper damage, mixed alloy components, high offset femoral stem, longer-length femoral head
- Hip osteoarthritis: increased water content, decreased proteoglycan content
  - o IL-1, IL-6, TNF-α increase matrix metalloprotease (MMP) activity → cartilage degeneration
  - o Osteophyte formation: Indian hedgehog (Ihh) mediates activation of chondrocyte differentiation → osteophyte formation (pathologic activation of endochondral ossification)
- Ideal position of acetabular component: abduction (40° +/- 10°), anteversion (15° +/- 10°)
  - o Increase ROM / stability by increasing head-neck ratio & femoral offset; skirt decreases head-neck ratio
- Bleeding under transverse acetabular ligament is from obturator artery
- Spinal anesthesia is most effective at reducing EBL & therefore postoperative transfusion requirement
- Pseudotumor is generally caused by fretting & corrosion reaction from taper

- After THA, safe to return to driving at 2 weeks
- Joint reactive forces: decrease by medializing acetabular component or increasing femoral offset.
  o Varus N-S stem (~127°): increases offset w/out increasing JRF or leg length
- Intraoperative periprosthetic femur fracture is highest when placing uncemented femoral stem via lateral approach
  o If calcar is fractured intraoperatively, remove stem, cable or wire calcar, followed by reinsertion of stem
- Intramedullary pressure (and thus risk for fat embolism) is highest during pressurization of cement
- Sickle cell anemia: risk of perforation of femoral canal during preparation because of sclerosis
- Trunnionosis: increased w/ larger head sizes (36 and 40mm)
  o Damage from galvanic corrosion between 2 dissimilar metals (e.g., titanium stem & CoCr head) or fretting from micromotion between 2 similar metals
- Metal-on-metal bearing: MRI with metal suppression to evaluate for pseudotumor
  o Monitor serum cobalt & chromium levels
- Quadrants: first line is from ASIS to center of acetabulum, second line is perpendicular to this
  o Posterosuperior: *safe zone*; sciatic nerve, superior gluteal nerve / vessels
  o Posteroinferior: sciatic nerve, inferior gluteal nerve / vessels
  o Anteroinferior: obturator nerve / vessels
  o Anterosuperior: death zone; external iliac vessels
- Posterior precautions: avoid hip flexion, adduction, IR
- Anterior precautions: avoid hip extension, adduction, ER
- Cement fixation: ideal cement mantle is >2mm
- Biologic fixation (rule of 50s): pore size 50-150µm, porosity 50%, gap <50µm, micromotion <150µm
- Sciatic nerve palsy: usually *peroneal division*; decrease tension by extending hip & flexing knee
  o Persistent foot drop: AFO
    ▪ If fails nonoperative treatment: posterior tibialis tendon

transfer
- Anterior overhang of acetabular component → iliopsoas impingement

Approach	Interval	Significance
Anterior (Smith-Petersen)	Superficial: sartorius (FN) & TFL (SGN) Deep: rectus femoris (FN) & GMed (SGN)	Between sartorius & TFL: LFCN & ascending branch of LFCA Lower dislocation rate than posterior
Anterolateral (Watson-Jones)	TFL (SGN) & GMed (SGN)	
Direct lateral (Hardinge)	Transgluteal	Proximal splitting of abductors risks injury to SGN → Trendelenburg gait • SGN is located between GMin & GMed 4-5cm above tip of greater trochanter Lower dislocation rate than posterior Higher HO
Posterior (Moore or Southern)		Injury to MFCA & perforating branch of profunda femoris Higher dislocation rate

5.2.3 Total hip revision
- In general, if components are well-positioned & well-fixed, leave alone (just address PE liner)
- Acetabular component: cementless reconstruction with porous hemispherical shell
- Abductor dysfunction & atrophy: gluteus maximus transfer
- Lateralized liner: moves COR laterally and reduces bony impingement but increases JRF

5.2.4 Hip resurfacing
- Metal-on-metal → pseudotumor
- Femoral neck notching → risk for periprosthetic FNF

5.3 KNEE

5.3.1 Primary total knee replacement

- Adductor canal block: preserves quad function compared to femoral nerve block and thus permits earlier ambulation following TKA
- No benefit over patient-specific designs vs standard symptoms
- AAOS recommends NSAIDs & tramadol for knee OA
  - Recommends against hyaluronic acid injection
  - Weight loss is most effective nonsurgical treatment
  - Recommends PT to start on day of surgery
  - New AAOS CPGs w/ *strong recommendation* on use of periarticular local anesthetic ("joint juice"); early supervised PT post-op w/ *moderate* recommendation; use of abx-cement w/ *limited* recommendation
- Knee arthritis leads to gait with increased knee adductor moment (KAM).
- Metal allergy can cause continued pain after TKA (although not increase rate of failure); rates of metal allergy: *Nickel* > Cobalt > Chrome
- As knee flexes, the center of pivot is medial (femoral condyle rollbacks around center of medial compartment) & tibia internally rotates (while femur externally rotates)
- Better alignment of components with medial parapatellar approach compared to quadriceps-sparing approaches
- Prior patellectomy & inflammatory arthritis: use posterior stabilized (PS) TKR systems.
  - Inflammatory arthritis is an absolute indication to resurface patella
- Neuropathic knee arthropathy: use constrained prosthesis (although more vulnerable to aseptic loosening)
- Infection is most common reason for revision within first 2 years after primary TKR; aseptic loosening is most common reason for revision after 2 years
- Arthrofibrosis after TKR: MUA before 3 months if knee flexion <90°; after 3 months, need surgical lysis of adhesions
  - Flexion contracture postoperative is due to hamstring tightness & spasm
- Metal tibial baseplate with PE insert: more backside PE wear

- If MCL is inadvertently cut during TKR, primary repair of MCL with sutures or suture anchors & brace postoperatively
- Most common intraoperative fracture is *medial* femoral condyle
- Weight loss (BMI <40) is best method to reduce risk for infection.
  - Smoking: major risk factor for periop infection &readmission w/in 90-day
- Bone cuts
  - Cutting tibia or changing PE size affects both flexion & extension gaps
  - Changing tibial slope affects flexion gap
    - Example: tight flexion, full extension → cut proximal tibia with increased tibial slope
  - Cutting distal femur affects only extension gap
    - Example: knee flexion contracture (tight in extension) → resect more bone from distal femur
  - Cutting posterior femur or changing femoral component size only affects flexion gap
- Cutting PCL increases flexion gap >>> extension gap
- TKR in a valgus knee
  - Tight in flexion on lateral side: release popliteus
  - Tight in extension on lateral side: release iliotibial band
- TKR in a varus knee: first step is deep MCL release
- Knee with valgus & flexion contracture has highest risk of peroneal nerve palsy after TKR
- Up to 20° in AP plane (coronal deformity) & lateral plane (sagittal deformity) can be corrected through intraarticular bone cuts during TKR
- All-poly tibia component w/ lower cost, lower risk of osteolysis, and equivalent or better clinical results and long-term survivorship vs modular metal-backed components
- Increasing Q angle causes patella maltracking
  - Q angle is increased with IR of femoral or tibial component, medializing femoral or tibial component & lateral placement of patellar prosthesis
  - Deflate tourniquet (if being used) for accurate assessment of maltracking
- History of high tibial osteotomy (HTO) → patella baja (Insall- Salvati

ratio <0.8)
- o TKR in patella baja: place patella component superiorly & lower joint line (cut less femur, cut more tibia)

5.3.2 Unicompartmental knee arthroplasty (UKA)
- Better knee biomechanics & earlier rehabilitation compared to TKR
- Contraindications: inflammatory arthritis, ACL deficiency, *fixed* sagittal or coronal deformity, symptomatic arthritis of multiple compartments
- Tibial plateau stress fracture is common problem.
- Good indication is for SPONK: 90% survival at 10 years

5.3.3 Patellar clunk syndrome
- *PS TKR*: scar tissue gets caught in cam (intercondylar notch) as knee is flexed; scar tissue then gets displaced as knee is extended, causing catching or clunking sensation.
  - o Synovial proliferation on undersurface of quad tendon adjacent to patella component
  - o Symptomatic → arthroscopic vs open resection
- Risk factors: older generation TKAs w/ wider boxes, undersized patellar component, over-resection of patella, low placement of patellar component

5.3.4 Total knee revision
- Tibial metaphyseal defect: tantalum trabecular metal cones are best at filling defect
- Per FDA, addition of abx to bone cement is only indicated in revision TKA (NOT indicated in primary TKA)
- MSIS major criteria for PJI: 1) draining sinus 2) two positive Cxs of same organism
- Anteromedial wound defects → medial gastric flap (medial sural artery)
  - o Medial gastric has more rotational excursion than lateral and is larger
- Extensor mechanisms failure: options are EM recon w/ allograft (CI in setting of infection), fusion (if adequate bone stock), or amp (if inadequate bone stock)
- For diagnosing PJI, synovial alpha-defensin and leukocyte esterase

reagent strips are most predictive

5.4 PERIPROSTHETIC

5.4.1 Aseptic loosening & osteolysis
- CT is best at estimating extent of osteolysis
- Osteolysis is mediated by macrophages
  - Macrophages release local factors TNFα → activation of osteoclasts & bone resorption
- Acetabular dysplasia: up to 30-40% of acetabular cup may be uncovered without increasing risk for aseptic loosening
- Offset liner leads to early acetabular component loosening
- Acetabular revision with adequate bone stock (small defect): porous-coated hemisphere cup
- Large acetabular defect/deficiency with pelvic discontinuity: custom triflange is better than reconstruction/antiprotrusio *cage*
- Paprosky classification of acetabular bone loss: type III is the worst & is associated with superior cup migration
  - IIIA: superolateral cup migration
  - IIIB: superomedial cup migration
- Femoral metaphyseal bone deficiency: need at least 4cm of good femoral diaphyseal bone to obtain scratch fit along femoral isthmus during revision THA (Paprosky type IIIA femoral defect)
  - If this is the case, can use extensively porous-coated diaphyseal fitting or tapered fluted stem; cementless systems

5.4.2 Periprosthetic fracture
- Acetabular fracture
  - If stable → protected weight bearing
  - If unstable → acetabular revision +/- ORIF
- Femur fracture
  - Vancouver B1: ORIF fracture with cerclage cables/wires & locking plates
  - Vancouver B2: ORIF fracture, then revise using fully porous coated cementless stem; make sure stem bypasses fracture by 2 cortical diameters

- o Vancouver B3: revision with proximal femoral replacement
- o Vancouver C: ORIF with locking plate extending at least 2
  cortical diameters above tip of femoral prosthesis
- Patella fracture: if extensor mechanism is intact, treat with cylinder cast
  or brace, WBAT
  - o Patella fracture with disrupted extensor mechanism: ORIF or
    revision
  - o Patellar or quadriceps tendon rupture → immobilization if
    partial (intact extensor mechanism), primary repair if complete
    - ▪ Chronic rupture, irreparable rupture or extensor lag
      → extensor mechanism reconstruction with allograft
- Periprosthetic distal femur fracture: locked plating has higher nonunion
  compared to retrograde IMN
  - o Plating of periprosthetic distal femur fracture: submuscular
    plating has lower nonunion rate than plating via extensile lateral
    approach
  - o Locked plating of distal femur: diabetes is a risk fracture for
    fixation failure
  - o Retrograde IMN only for cruciate retaining TKR design; not for
    closed-box posterior stabilized TKR design
    - ▪ *Arthrotomy* during retrograde IMN allows visualization
      & protection of polyethylene liner
  - o In general, if TKR tibial or femoral component is well-fixed &
    stable → surgical fixation of fracture; if loose → revision to
    long stem prosthesis
    - ▪ If patient is elderly with osteoporotic bone, distal
      femoral replacement may be a better option than surgical
      fixation to allow early weight bearing

5.4.3 Periprosthetic infection

- After total joint replacement, prophylaxis with amoxicillin or
  cephalexin given 1 hour before dental procedure for first 2 years
  postoperative
- Definition of surgical site infection (SSI): if surgery involves retaining
  hardware → SSI is within 365 days; if no hardware is retained → within
  30 days
- Reduce risk by minimizing allogenous blood transfusion

- CRP is most sensitive test for identifying postsurgical infection
  - CRP normally trends down after postoperative day 2
- Can test for *alpha defensin* or *leukocyte esterase* level in synovial fluid: alpha defensin is antimicrobial peptide secreted by neutrophils
- Acute PJI: within 4 weeks postoperative
  - Aspirate: within 6 weeks after primary TKR, synovial WBC 27,800 cells/uL has 95% predictive value of PJI
  - I&D with liner exchange
- Chronic PJI: after 4 weeks
  - Aspirate: WBC >1,100 cells/uL for TKR, >3,000 cells/uL for THA; PMN >64% for TKR, >80% for THA
  - Stage I: resection arthroplasty; stage II: revision joint replacement when infection clears

DOMAIN 6: FOOT & ANKLE

6.1 BASICS

6.1.1 Gait biomechanics
- Toe off during terminal stance: posterior tibialis fires causing subtalar inversion, which locks transverse tarsal joints, stabilizing hindfoot/midfoot for push off
  - o Posterior tibialis is most important during terminal stance stage of gait cycle
- Heel strike (early stance): subtalar eversion unlocks transverse tarsal joints → supple foot acts as shock absorber as foot contacts ground
- During gait cycle, anterior tibialis *eccentrically* contracts as ankle plantarflexes, then *concentrically* contracts as ankle dorsiflexes
- Quadriceps weakness will cause knee hyperextension during swing phase
  - o Weakness of hip flexors affects limb advancement during swing phase.
- During ankle dorsiflexion, fibula pistons proximally and ER within incisura

6.1.2 Ankle arthroscopy
- Most common complication is neurapraxia
  - o Anterolateral portal: SPN
  - o Anteromedial portal: saphenous nerve & vein

6.1.3 Diabetic foot
- Initial treatment of diabetic ulcer without signs of infection → total contact casting
  - o If there is Achilles or gastrocnemius contracture → consider tendo-Achilles lengthening (TAL) or gastrocnemius recession
- Better healing is associated with: albumin >3, ABI >0.45, lymphocyte count >1,500, toe pressure >40, transcutaneous oxygen tension >30
- Chronic plantar ulcer at IP joint of hallux: if no sign of infection → Keller arthroplasty

- Chronic heel ulcer unresponsive to serial debridement, probe-to- bone or osteomyelitis on MRI
  - Adequate perfusion: calcaneal saucerization (partial or total calcanectomy) & TAL
  - Inadequate perfusion: below knee amputation
- Chronic plantar forefoot ulcer: Strayer or TAL
- Charcot (neuropathic) arthropathy: limb elevation will reduce hyperemia (vs infection)
  - Pathophysiology: bone destruction is due to *hypervascularity* of bone
  - Technetium bone scan: positive for neuropathic arthropathy & osteomyelitis
  - Indium WBC scan: only positive for osteomyelitis
  - Initial treatment of active Charcot arthropathy is total contact casting, then transition to CROW
  - Neuropathic arthropathy of glenohumeral joint: obtain C- spine MRI to rule out syringomyelia

6.2 DEFORMITY

6.2.1 Hallux valgus
- Hallux is plantarflexed, pronated & in valgus
- Normal angles: HVA <15°, IMA <9°, DMAA <10°
- HVA ≤40°, IMA <13°: distal MT osteotomy
- HVA >40°, IMA >13°: proximal MT osteotomy or combined proximal/distal MT osteotomies
  - If there is increased DMAA: combined proximal/distal MT osteotomies (need to do distal MT osteotomy to correct DMAA)
- Symptomatic 1st TMT arthritis or instability: 1st TMT arthrodesis (Lapidus procedure)
  - Instability is characterized by medial translation & plantar gapping of 1st TMTJ on xrays
- Dorsomedial cutaneous nerve (branch of SPN) is at risk with hallux valgus surgery
- Modified McBride procedure includes release of *adductor hallucis* to help correct deformity

- Hallux valgus interphalangeus: proximal phalanx (Akin) osteotomy
- Hallux valgus in patients with advanced MTP arthritis or neuromuscular conditions: MTP fusion
- Excessive resection of medial eminence (excessive lateral placement of sagittal saw blade) → iatrogenic hallux varus
- Juvenile or adolescent hallux valgus: open physis so perform *medial cuneiform osteotomy* rather than MT osteotomy

6.2.2 Hallux rigidus
- Carbon shank with Morton's extension
- Mild hallux rigidus, pain only with terminal dorsiflexion: dorsal cheilectomy
  - Dorsiflexion is most limited ROM with hallux rigidus
- Advanced hallux rigidus, pain throughout ROM: MTP fusion
  - Low demand, elderly patient: MTP resection (Keller) arthroplasty
  - Most reliable reference to determine position for MTP fusion is simulated weight bearing on a flat surface
- Salvage for failed 1st MTP surgeries (such as hemiarthroplasty or total arthroplasty): arthrodesis with structural bone graft (distraction bone block arthrodesis)
- Interposition arthroplasty vs fusion: IPA w/ synthetic cartilage implant ("Cartiva") w/ few postop WB restrictions, equivalent pain reduction, decreased surgical time, maintained ROM
  - Not recommended in pts w/ hallux varus/valgus >20°
  - More prolonged time to *maximum* pain reduction compared to fusion

6.2.3 Bunionette
- Type I: enlarged 5th MT head +/- lateral exostosis
  - Exostectomy (lateral condylectomy) of 5th MT head
- Type II: lateral bowing of 5th MT
  - Distal chevron osteotomy of 5th MT
- Type III: widened 4,5 intermetatarsal angle (>12°)

      o Rotational diaphyseal osteotomy of 5th MT

6.2.4 Cavovarus foot deformity

- Require full neurologic workup/exam as this is commonly associated with neurologic conditions such as CMTD, Freidreich's ataxia, cerebral palsy, spinal cord pathologies
- Peroneal longus overpowers anterior tibialis (*predominant* deforming force) → cavus
- Posterior tibialis overpowers peroneal brevis → varus
- Initial deformity is usually plantarflexion of 1st ray
- Full-length insert with 1st MT head recess & lateral heel and sole wedge
- Coleman block test
  - Flexible deformity (positive Coleman block test): plantar fascia release (tight plantar fascia contributes to cavus deformity), PT tendon transfer to dorsum of foot, PL transfer to PB, TAL, 1st MT dorsiflexion osteotomy
  - Rigid deformity (negative Coleman block test): lateralizing calcaneal osteotomy

6.2.5 Flatfoot (pes planovalgus)

- Pediatric flexible flatfoot: if fails nonoperative treatment → varus producing calcaneal osteotomy (calcaneal lengthening osteotomy or medializing calcaneal osteotomy)
- Adult acquired flatfoot
  - Posterior tibial tendon insufficiency (PTTI) results in inability to "lock" transverse tarsal joints during push off (unable to perform single limb heel rise): pathomechanics of calf pain with walking
  - Spring (calcaneonavicular) ligament becomes attenuated
  - Nonoperative: AFO or insert with medial arch support / medial post
  - Lateral hindfoot pain due to *lateral impaction syndrome*: subluxation of talocalcaneal joint → impingement between talus & calcaneus in sinus tarsi and/or distal fibula & calcaneus

Stage	Deformity	Radiograph	Operative
I	None, able to perform single limb heel rise	Normal	--
II	Flexible planovalgus, unable to perform single limb heel rise	Flatfoot	*FDL transfer* to augment posterior tibialis, varus-producing *calcaneal osteotomy* (medializing or lateral column lengthening)
III	Rigid planovalgus	Subtalar arthritis	*Arthrodesis* that includes subtalar arthrodesis (e.g., triple arthrodesis)
IV	Rigid planovalgus	Talar tilt (failure of deltoid ligament)	*Arthrodesis* that also addresses talar tilt (e.g., TTC arthrodesis)

- Residual forefoot varus deformity (due to malposition of transverse tarsal joint): dorsal opening plantarflexion (Cotton) osteotomy of medial cuneiform
- Lateral column lengthening corrects forefoot abduction & talonavicular subluxation
- Reduce infection risk by performing subtalar & talonavicular arthrodesis through single medial approach
- Small subset of patients with acquired flatfoot deformity due to midfoot arthritis or instability (i.e., normal PT function) → midfoot arthrodesis & TAL
- **Silfverskiold test**
    - ○ >10° increase in ankle dorsiflexion with knee flexed compared to knee extended → gastrocnemius tightness (Silfverskiold positive) → gastrocnemius recession
    - ○ <10° increase in ankle dorsiflexion with knee flexed compared to knee extended → Achilles tightness (Silfverskiold negative) → Achilles tendon lengthening
- TTC fusion with IMN: lateral plantar nerve is at greatest risk

6.2.6 Spastic equinovarus foot deformity
- Usually after stroke or traumatic brain injury → spastic GSC causes equinus; spastic tibialis anterior causes varus
- If nonoperative treatment fails (e.g., AFO): TAL & split anterior tibialis tendon transfer (SPLATT) to cuboid

6.3 FOOT PATHOLOGIES

6.3.1 5th metatarsal fracture
- Zone 1: WBAT
- Zone 2 (Jones, watershed area) or 3 (fracture distal to intermetatarsal joint): NWB in short leg cast in most patients
  - o High-level athletes: intramedullary screw fixation (solid preferred over cannulated screw)
    - ▪ No return to play prior to radiographic union

6.3.2 Interdigital (Morton's) neuroma
- Risk factor: narrow toe box shoes
- Diagnosis is made entirely on H&P
- Interdigital nerve runs *below* transverse intermetatarsal ligament
- Mulder click on exam
- Need to rule out other causes of pain → MTP instability
- Nonoperative (wide shoe box & metatarsal pad, cortisone injection) → operative (dorsal neurectomy)
  - o Multiple cortisone injections can lead to development of hammertoe deformity
  - o Most common complication after neurectomy is persistent pain due to inadequate resection
- Histology: perineural fibrosis

6.3.3 2nd MTP synovitis
- Walking on a "marble", callus under 2nd MT head with tenderness to palpation over 2nd MTP joint, subluxation with drawer test (i.e., dorsal subluxation of MTP joint)
- Deficiency of plantar plate → cross-over toe deformity

113

- Foot orthotic with metatarsal pad is initial treatment
- Fixed dorsal MTP dislocation due to long MT: distal oblique MT shortening (Weil) osteotomy

6.3.4 Hammertoe
- Overpull of EDL & contracture of FDL → PIP flexion & DIP extension
- Fails nonoperative treatment (e.g., shoe with high, broad toe box)
  - Flexible deformity: FDL to EDL transfer
  - Rigid deformity: PIP resection arthroplasty (resect P1 head & neck)

6.3.5 Mallet toe
- DIP hyperflexion from FDL contracture
- Fails nonoperative treatment (e.g., shoe modification, toe sleeve)
  - Flexible deformity: FDL tenotomy or FDL transfer to dorsum of phalanx
  - Rigid deformity: DIP fusion or DIP resection arthroplasty (resect P2)

6.3.6 Claw toe
- Intrinsic minus foot deformity: MTP hyperextension, PIP/DIP flexion
- Usually due to MTP synovitis → attenuation of plantar plate
- Nonoperative treatment: taping
- Operative
  - Flexible deformity: EDB tenotomy, EDL lengthening, FDL flexor-to-extensor transfer
  - Fixed deformity: resection arthroplasty of proximal phalanx or distal MT (Weil) osteotomy
    - Most common complication of Weil osteotomy is floating toe (dorsiflexion deformity of MTP)

6.3.7 Turf toe
- Hyperextension injury of 1st MTP joint, resulting in injury to plantar plate & sesamoid complex
  - Xrays may show proximal migration of sesamoids compared to contralateral foot

- o Weight bearing foot xrays or forced dorsiflexion xrays of hallux can be helpful
  - However, if unable to bear weight or too symptomatic for forced dorsiflexion xrays → *MRI* of forefoot
- Acute injury in non-athlete: stabilization taping
  - o Athlete: plantar plate repair

6.3.8 Sesamoid fracture
- Sesamoids are embedded in FHB tendon
- If fails nonoperative treatment (boot or cast immobilization) → sesamoidectomy
  - o Tibial sesamoidectomy → hallux valgus deformity
  - o Fibular sesamoidectomy → hallux varus deformity
  - o Sesamoidectomy of both → cock-up hallux deformity due to weakness of FHB

6.3.9 Navicular stress fracture
- White-out on T2 MRI suggests complete fracture line or nonunion / AVN
  - o Obtain CT scan: if there is a complete fracture line or nonunion / AVN, consider surgery especially in an athlete
- Cast immobilization, NWB for 6 weeks
- Osteonecrosis of navicular (Kohler disease): immobilization in short leg walking cast if symptomatic

6.3.10 Heel pain

Condition	Physical exam	Overview	Treatment
Baxter nerve (first branch of lateral plantar nerve)	Pain in plantar medial heel (over abductor hallucis origin) **AND** base of 5th metatarsal (+Tinel's radiating to lateral forefoot)	Innervates abductor digiti quinti; compression between abductor hallucis longus & quadratus plantae	Release fascia of abductor hallucis longus
Plantar fasciitis	Tight GSC, TTP over medial process of calcaneal tuberosity	Pain is worse when first getting out of bed, better after a few steps, worse again at end of day • If rupture after cortisone injection → cast immobilization • Multiple injections can lead to heel pad atrophy → shoe wear modifications • BMI >30 is a risk factor	Eccentric stretching of plantar fascia & Achilles, night splint → shock wave → plantar fasciotomy, Strayer or TAL
Tarsal tunnel syndrome	Tinel sign with percussion of tibial nerve	Paresthesias in plantar foot with compression of tarsal tunnel	If fails nonoperative → tarsal tunnel release
Calcaneus stress fracture	Pain with compression of calcaneus		Immobilization

6.3.11 Anterior tarsal tunnel syndrome

- Tight shoe (e.g., ski boot)
- Entrapment of DPN at level of inferior extensor retinaculum
- Pain & paresthesias in DPN distribution (1st web space), Tinel's sign
  - o Tenderness to palpation over 1st & 2nd MT bases
- If fails nonoperative treatment → release inferior extensor retinaculum

6.3.12 Achilles tendinosis

- *Eccentric* closed-chain stretching program
- Achilles tendon debridement with calcaneal exostectomy (excision of Haglund's deformity)
  - o If >50% of Achilles insertion is debrided or if >50% of Achilles tendon is debrided, augment Achilles via FHL (best option) or FDL transfer.
    - ▪ FHL transfer has no effect on VAS pain scores, clinical outcome scores, patient satisfaction, or hallux plantarflexion strength (compared to w/out); but it does result in *increased ankle plantarflexion strength*
- Achilles tendinosis with chronic attritional rupture: calcaneal ostectomy & insertional repair

6.3.13 Achilles rupture

- Higher risk of re-rupture with nonoperative management
- Early motion after operative or nonoperative treatment decreases rerupture rate.
- <2cm: mobilization of proximal stump + end-to-end repair
- 2-5cm: above +/- VY advancement
- Chronic rupture, gap >5 cm: Gastrocnemius turndown reconstruction +/- FHL tendon transfer

6.3.14 Os trigonum

- Posterior ankle impingement (os is impinged between posterior malleolus & calcaneal tuberosity) with maximum plantarflexion (especially ballet dancers)
- FHL lies adjacent to os & therefore FHL tendonitis is commonly

associated with os trigonum
- Os trigonum (posterolateral ankle pain) vs FHL tendinitis (posteromedial ankle pain, triggering of hallux)
- Fails nonoperative treatment: open vs posterior ankle arthroscopic resection
    - Posterior ankle arthroscopy puts *sural nerve* at risk

6.3.15 Tarsal coalition
- Calcaneonavicular is more common than talocalcaneal coalition
- Flatfoot (planovalgus), recurrent ankle sprains
- Symptomatic → immobilization in short-leg cast
- Resection with interposition of fat or EDB
    - Calcaneonavicular: lateral incision over sinus tarsi
    - Talocalcaneal: medial incision between FDL & FHL (at level of sustentaculum tali)

6.4 ANKLE PATHOLOGIES

6.4.1 Ankle sprain
- High ankle sprain (syndesmotic injury): AITFL is initial ligament of syndesmosis to be injured
- Low ankle sprain (ATFL & CFL injury):
    - ATFL is injured during plantarflexion & inversion: laxity to anterior drawer test in plantarflexion
    - CFL is injured during dorsiflexion & inversion: laxity to anterior drawer test in dorsiflexion
    - Acute ligamentous injury: immobilization for 7-10 days followed by functional rehab & proprioceptive retraining
        - Do not get MRI acutely

6.4.2 Osteochondral lesion of talus (OLT)
- Lateral lesions are usually traumatic; medial lesions are more common
- Acute lesion: short leg cast immobilization
- Displaced OCD: microfracture, OAT or ACI depending on size of OCD
- OCD with intact cartilage cap: retrograde drilling & bone graft

6.4.3 Peroneal tendon subluxation / dislocation
- Superior peroneal retinaculum (SPR) is injured with forced ankle dorsiflexion & *inversion*
    o Subluxation is reproducible (apprehension test) with ankle dorsiflexion & *eversion* against resistance
- Repair of superior peroneal retinaculum (SPR) & deepening of fibular groove
- Peroneal tendon tear
    o Small tears: debridement, core repair & tubularization
    o Large irreparable tear of one tendon: tenodesis to intact tendon
    o Large irreparable tears of both tendons: FHL transfer or allograft reconstruction
        ▪ Allograft reconstruction requires proximal muscle excursion
- PB is on bone (fibula; anterior to PL), broader/more ribbon-shaped, and has more distal muscle belly relative to PL
    o Trick: think of PL as "posterolateral" to PB

6.4.4 Ankle arthritis
- Post-traumatic arthritis following ankle fx is thought secondary to 1) direct cartilage injury and 2) increase in proinflammatory CKs and MMPs in synovial fluid that contribute to cartilage degradation
- To preserve option for future TAA during fusion, do anterior approach (spare the fibula)
- Nonoperative: cortisone injection, Arizona AFO, single rocker sole shoe
- Operative: ankle arthrodesis is best answer on OITE
    o High rate of subtalar arthritis after ankle arthrodesis
    o Fuse ankle in neutral dorsiflexion, 5-10° ER, 5° hindfoot valgus
    o Using a heel-to-toe rocker sole can dissipate forces across arthrodesis
    o Advanced peripheral neuropathy w/ insensate foot is hard contraindication against arthroplasty (do fusion instead)
        ▪ Ipsilateral hindfoot arthritis is also indication for fusion over arthroplasty
        ▪ Focal AVN of talus is not a contraindication for either
- Isolated anterior tibiotalar impingement from osteophytes
    o If fails conservative treatment → open vs arthroscopic anterior

ankle cheilectomy / debridement

6.4.5 Total ankle replacement
- TAR increases stride length, cadence & velocity compared to fusion
- Acute infection (within 4 weeks after TAR): I&D with PE exchange
- Chronic infection (> 4 weeks after TAR): I&D, explant, staged ankle fusion with structural graft
- Failed TAR: salvage is ankle fusion with structural graft

DOMAIN 7: SPINE

7.1 BASICS

7.1.1 Cervical spine anatomy

Nerve root	Motor	Sensory	Reflex
C5	Deltoid, biceps	Lateral shoulder/arm	Biceps
C6	Brachioradialis, ECRL	Thumb	Brachioradialis
C7	Triceps, FCR	Long finger	Triceps
C8	FDS	Small finger	
T1	Interossei	Medial elbow	

7.1.2 Lumbar spine anatomy

Nerve root	Motor	Sensory	Reflex
L2, L3	Iliopsoas, hip adductors	Anterior & medial thigh	
L4	*Quadriceps*, TA	Anterior knee, medial leg	Patellar
L5	*EHL*, TA, TP, hamstrings, glutei	Lateral leg, dorsal foot	
S1	GSC, peroneals	Posterior leg	Achilles
S2	FHL, FDL	Plantar foot	
S3, S4	Bowel & bladder	Perianal	

- Spinal cord normally extends to L2

7.1.3 Approach-related complications
- Anterior cervical spine
  - Recurrent laryngeal nerve → hoarseness
  - Sympathetic nerves → Horner's syndrome
- Posterior cervical spine
  - Wound infection

- o   C5 palsy
- ALIF
  - o   Superior hypogastric plexus: retrograde ejaculation →
        infertility
  - o   Sympathetic trunk: anhidrosis; one leg feels colder than the
        other (damage to sympathetic trunk leads to vasodilation of
        cutaneous BVs → increased temperature of affected extremity)
- Lateral LIF
  - o   Ilioinguinal nerve: travels with round ligament / spermatic cord
        through superficial inguinal ring
  - o   Iliohypogastric nerve
- Wiltse approach (for far lateral herniation): between longissimus and
  multifidus

7.1.4 Spinal cord injury (SCI)

- STIR sequences best show acute traumatic injury
- Central cord: hyperextension injury
  - o   Lateral corticospinal tracts of upper extremities are more central
        → upper extremities are more affected than lower extremities in
        central cord syndrome
- Anterior cord: injury to anterior spinal artery, which supplies anterior
  $2/3^{rd}$ of spinal cord
  - o   Loss of motor (corticospinal tract) & pain/temperature sensation
        (spinothalamic tract), preserved proprioception/vibration
        sensation (dorsal columns)
- Brown-Sequard: cord hemitransection
  - o   Loss of ipsilateral motor & proprioception/vibration sensation &
        contralateral pain/temperature sensation
- Athlete with suspected SCI: can remove facemask to assess airway but
  leave helmet/shoulder pads on until able to safely apply c-collar
- NASCIS guidelines
  - o   Give methylprednisone only within *8 hours* of injury
  - o   If administered <3 hrs after injury: methylprednisone for 24 hrs
  - o   If administered between 3-8 hours after injury:
        methylprednisone for 48 hrs

- Distended bowel or bladder will stimulate autonomic dysreflexia after SCI: HTN, sweating, piloerection, facial flushing, headache, blurred vision, stuffy nose
  - Treatment: urinary catheterization, bowel disimpaction & treat HTN
- Functional electrical stimulation mechanism of action: direct stimulation of skeletal muscles
- Lumbar SCI (conus medullaris) has highest potential for neurologic improvement

7.1.5 ASIA Classification

Grade	Type of SCI	Description
A	Complete	No motor or sensory function below level of injury
B	Incomplete	Sensory function preserved, no motor function
C	Incomplete	More than half of muscles involved have grade <3
D	Incomplete	More than half of muscles involved have grade ≥3
E	Normal	Normal sensorimotor function

- ASIA Grade has *highest* effect on cost of care

7.1.6 Disc herniation

- Cervical disc herniation: cervical nerve root exits *above* corresponding pedicle
  - All cervical disc herniation types affect same nerve root
- Lumbar disc herniation: lumbar nerve root exits *below* corresponding pedicle
  - Central & paracentral: impinges traversing (lower) nerve root
  - Foraminal & extraforaminal: impinges exiting (upper) nerve root
    - Extraforaminal: Wiltse approach (between longissimus & multifidus) for far-lateral discectomy
- Disc will resorb over time via phagocytosis by macrophages
- Symptomatic after discectomy, MRI with *gadolinium* to differentiate between fibrosis (contrast enhancing) vs recurrent disc herniation (non-

enhancing)
- o Revision discectomy has similar outcomes compared to primary discectomy

7.1.7 Vertebral compression fracture
- Acute fracture: low on T1, high on STIR / T2
- Treatment is generally nonoperative *without* need for bracing
- AAOS recommends *against* vertebroplasty
- Prior compression fracture is highest predictor of future spinal fragility fractures

7.1.8 Ankylosing disease of the spine
- If suspected fracture but negative xrays, obtain CT
  - o If fracture, *long* fusion construct (posterior arthrodesis)
- DISH: diabetes
  - o Nonmarginal syndesmophytes (flowing ossification)
  - o Disc space is not involved
  - o DISH most commonly affects *right* side of *thoracic* spine
  - o THA in DISH: higher risk of heterotopic ossification
  - o DISH in C-spine can cause dysphagia—common associated complaint
  - o Associated with enthesophytes (Achilles tendinopathy common)
- Ankylosing spondylitis: HLA-B27, sacroiliitis (positive FABER test), enthesitis, has *pain* usually (whereas DISH is typically painless)
  - o *Marginal* syndesmophytes, vertebral scalloping (bamboo spine)
  - o Disc space is also ossified
  - o Kyphotic (chin-on-chest) deformity: C7-T1 posterior extension osteotomy & instrumented fusion; deformity precludes anterior approach
  - o THA in AS (even after posterior approach): *anterior* >>> posterior dislocation because of relative hyperextension of hip after THA

7.2 CERVICAL

7.2.1 Atlantoaxial instability
- Transverse ligament is most important stabilizer

- o Rule of Spence: combined C1 lateral mass overhang >6.9mm (or >8.1mm with radiographic magnification) indicates disruption of transverse ligament
  - Atlanto-dens interval (ADI) >3.5mm in adult & >5mm in pediatric is unstable
  - Space available for cord (SAC) (aka posterior atlanto-dens interval or PADI) <13mm is associated with increased risk of neurologic injury

7.2.2 Cervical spine fracture
- Odontoid fracture: type I (avulsion of apical ligament), type II (watershed zone, junction of dens & body), type III (extension in C2 body)
  - o Type I & III: c-collar
  - o Type II: 30-day mortality of 15%, 50% at 2.5 years.
    - Young, small displacement (low risk of nonunion): c-collar
    - Elder, large displacement (high risk of nonunion): posterior C1-2 fusion
      - Aberrant vertebral artery is a contraindication to C1-2 transarticular screws
  - o Normal C2 osteology
    - Subdental (basilar) synchondrosis (between dens & vertebral body) fuses between 3-6 years of age
    - Secondary ossification center fuses at 12 years of age; failure to close → os odontoideum
- Hangman's fracture (bilateral C2 pars fracture → spondylolisthesis of C2 on C3): usually nonoperative (i.e., rigid cervical collar)
- Cervical facet fracture-dislocation
  - o Normal anatomy: superior facet is *anterior* to inferior facet
  - o Unilateral facet dislocation (25% listhesis) vs bilateral facet dislocation (50% listhesis)
  - o Cervical spine facet fracture dislocation / subluxation: highest incidence of vertebral artery injury
- Halo pin: 1cm above lateral one-third of orbit at equator of skull to avoid supraorbital nerve
  - o Cranial nerve 6 (abducens nerve) palsy: palsy of lateral rectus → loss of lateral gaze → diplopia

- Pediatric cervical spine trauma
  - Transporting on a standard adult backboard will flex neck (due to large occiput in children)
    - Need an occipital recess or pad from shoulders down (to elevate rest of body relative to head/neck)
  - Implementing pediatric cervical spine clearance guidelines decreases CT scan usage

7.2.3 Cervical spinal stenosis
- Myelopathy is a stepwise deterioration over time
- Contraindication to *posterior-only* decompression fusion procedure: fixed C2-C7 kyphosis (>13°)
- C5 is the most common nerve palsy postoperatively
- OPLL with adequate cervical lordosis: posterior laminoplasty or laminectomy with instrumented fusion (generally should avoid going anteriorly due to high risk of durotomy)
- Dysphagia is common after ACDF & usually resolves with time
- Symptomatic pseudarthrosis after ACDF → *posterior* instrumented fusion
- If suspect recurrent laryngeal nerve (RLN) palsy after ACDF: direct laryngoscopy to confirm & evaluate extent of injury
  - If anterior-based revision is required, approach from same side with known RLN palsy to avoid injuring contralateral RLN

7.2.4 Cervical radiculopathy
- Shoulder abduction test: abduction improves radicular symptoms
- Radicular arm pain without sensorimotor deficits or myelopathy: nonoperative treatment first
- Athlete with acute cervical radiculopathy: oral methylprednisolone will expedite return to play

7.2.5 Rheumatoid arthritis of cervical spine
- Pannus formation at atlantodental joint compromises transverse ligament → atlantoaxial subluxation
  - ADI >10mm or PADI/SAC <14mm is indication for posterior C1-2 decompression fusion
    - PADI/SAC >13mm is good prognostic indicator for

neurologic recovery after surgery
- Basilar invagination with cervical myelopathy: posterior occiput-C2 decompression fusion

7.3 LUMBAR

7.3.1 Thoracolumbar trauma
- Burst fracture: compression fracture of anterior & middle columns → retropulsion of posterior vertebral body into canal
  - o Lamina fracture is associated with traumatic dural tear
  - o Burst fracture without neurologic deficits: nonoperative treatment with TLSO
  - o Burst fracture with neurologic deficits: decompression & stabilization
- Chance's fracture: flexion distraction mechanism
  - o Associated with GI injuries
  - o Chance's fractures are generally unstable → decompression & stabilization regardless of neurologic function
- Thoracolumbar Injury Classification and Severity Score (TLICS): (1) fracture morphology, (2) neurologic status, (3) PLC integrity

7.3.2 Cauda equina
- Compression of cauda equina leads to lower motor neuron symptoms
  - o Neurogenic bladder: urinary retention → *overflow* incontinence
- Decompression within 48 hrs after onset of symptoms

7.3.3 Lumbar spinal stenosis
- SPORT trial: stenosis treated w/ surgery > non-operative management
  - o 3 domains studied: disc herniation, spinal stenosis, degen spondy w/ stenosis → surgery is better than non-op
    - ▪ Not examined w/ SPORT trial: adult deformity
- Neurogenic claudication: leg pain improves when leaning forward
  - o Neurologic exam is generally normal
- Vascular claudication: leg pain improves when standing still; always check peripheral pulses when evaluating a patient with lumbar spinal stenosis

- High rate of depression in patients undergoing lumbar spine surgery
- Synovial facet cyst can cause lumbar radiculopathy and/or neurogenic claudication
  - Refractory to nonoperative treatment: laminectomy & excision
    - High recurrence with laminectomy & excision; can consider facetectomy & fusion to prevent motion across facet joints (lowest risk for persistent back pain & recurrence of cyst)

7.3.4 Spondylolisthesis
- Degenerative spondylolisthesis: L4-5
- Isthmic spondylolisthesis: pars defect, L5-S1
  - Reduction of L5-S1 isthmic spondylolisthesis: L5 is at greatest risk of injury.
    - Compression at extraforaminal zone at site of pars hypertrophy
  - Main risk factor for slip progression is *age*
- Posterior decompression (laminectomy) & *instrumented* fusion
  - Laminectomy adjacent to posterior lumbar fusion is a major risk factor for adjacent segment degeneration (ASD)
- Pelvic incidence (PI) is correlated with isthmic spondylolisthesis
  - Pelvic incidence (PI) = pelvic tilt (PT) + sacral slope (SS)

7.3.5 Miscellaneous
- Adult deformity surgery
  - Age >60 years is highest risk factor for major perioperative complications
  - Venous thromboembolic event is associated with poor clinical outcomes
  - Sagittal imbalance is correlated with severity of symptoms
    - Goal SVA < 50mm, PT < 25 deg, correct LL within 10 deg pelvic incidence (remember: PI is fixed)
    - In general, correct sagittal alignment by changing *lumbar lordosis*
  - Scoliosis: spinal stenosis is worse on concave side
- Lumbar disc replacement
  - Symptomatic after lumbar disc replacement: posterior fusion is

      best salvage option
- Back pain: cognitive behavioral therapy (CBT) provides equivalent outcomes to lumbar instrumented fusion
- UMNS: spastic paresis, hyperreflexia, +Babinski
- LMNS: flaccid paralysis, hyporeflexia, muscle atrophy, fasciculation / fibrillation
  - Patient with UMNS, spinal stenosis on lumbar spine MRI: obtain full spine MRI to evaluate for tandem spinal stenosis
- Halo pin in skeletally immature patient: 8 pins at 2-4 in-lbs of torque— "finger tight"; vs adult: 4 pins at 6-8 in-lbs of torque
- Scheuermann kyphosis: increased thoracic kyphosis w/ wedging of vertebra
  - Possible link w/ Vitamin D deficiency
  - HLA-B27 is an *MHC Ag* linked to various seronegative arthritides such as this and Reiter's, psoriatic arthropathy
- Artery of Adamkiewicz: most commonly arises left T9-T11 intercostal arteries
- Intervertebral disc innervated by *sinu-vertebral nerve*
- Decrease in SSEP itself w/out latency changes is not indicative of intraop SCI; for SCI, need *latency drop of 50-60%*
- Pedicle electrical stimulation threshold of *8 milliAmps* or greater indicates intact pedicle; lower may signal pedicle breach
- Epidural hematoma acuity can be determined via MRI (oxygenation of Hb in hematoma changes, thus different signal intensities)
  - Hyperacute: hypointense T1, hyperintense T2
  - Subacute: deoxyHb converts to metHb and becomes hyperintense on T1
  - Chronic (>2 weeks): extracellular metHb converts to hemosiderin and is hypointense on both T1/T2

7.4 SPINE INFECTION

7.4.1 Spine osteomyelitis & epidural abscess
- Spondylodiskitis: disc space narrowing & endplate erosion are common with pyogenic osteomyelitis but not with tuberculosis or neoplasm
  - Most common in *L-spine (50-60%)* > T-spine (20-30%) > C-spine (20%); rare in sacrum
- Best study is MRI with & without gadolinium

- Antibiotics without biopsy if *positive* blood cultures
  - Otherwise, obtain IR-guided biopsy first, then give antibiotics
- Surgery if neurologic deterioration, refractory to antibiotics, or spinal deformity/instability
  - Since infection often involves vertebral body or disc (anterior structures), surgery usually requires *anterior* decompression & fusion +/- posterior instrumented fusion
- Pott's disease (spinal tuberculosis): severe focal spinal kyphosis; acid-fast bacilli (AFB)
- Pediatric diskitis: loss of lumbar lordosis is earliest radiographic finding

DOMAIN 8: ONCOLOGY

8.1 BASICS

8.1.1 Biopsy principles
- Longitudinal incision (extensile), intramuscular plane (single compartment), avoid joint penetration / contamination
  - *Best* incision is in *line with intended future resection*
- Proximal humerus: biopsy through anterior third of deltoid
- In general, go for core needle biopsy; if inadequate sample for diagnosis, then perform incisional biopsy
  - Avoid fine needle aspiration or excisional biopsy (marginal resection)

8.1.2 Chemoradiation
- Preoperative XRT: higher wound complications, less radiation (smaller field)
- Postoperative XRT: more radiation (larger field), fibrosis
- Conventional radiation: *photon therapy*
- *Proton beam therapy*: avoids exit dose and those used in spinal column tumors or tumors near spine
- Cryotherapy: known complication is fracture

Drug	Significance
Doxorubicin	Cardiac toxicity (CHF, cardiomyopathy)
Pazopanib	Mechanism: anti-VEGF

8.1.3 Genetics

Tumor	Genetics
Atypical lipomatous tumor (ALT, or well-differentiated liposarcoma)	MDM2 amplification
Myxoid liposarcoma	t(12;16), TLS-CHOP
Synovial sarcoma	t(X;18), SYT-SSX
Ewing sarcoma	t(11;22), EWS-FLI
Rhabdomyosarcoma	t(2;13), PAX-FKHR
Clear cell sarcoma	t(12;22), EWS-ATF
Myxoid chondrosarcoma	t(9;22), EWS-CHN

- Infantile fibrosarcoma: NTRK mutation
- Cytogenetic analysis determines translocation

8.1.4 Tumor markers

Tumor	Marker
Colorectal	CEA
Pancreatic	CA-19-1
Ovarian	CA-125
Breast	CA-15-3
HCC	AFP

8.2 BONE TUMORS

8.2.1 Fibrous dysplasia
- Activating missense mutation of Gs alpha protein (GNAS1 gene) →
  increased cAMP production
- Xrays: lytic lesions with ground-glass appearance
- Fibrous dysplasia of proximal femur → Shepherd's crook deformity
- McCune Albright: coast of Maine café au lait lesions, precocious
  puberty, polyostotic fibrous dysplasia
- Histology: "alphabet soup"; fibroblasts surrounding islands of osteoid;
  no osteoblastic rimming

8.2.2 Nonossifying fibroma (NOF)
- Eccentric "soap bubbles" lesion in metaphysis, thin sclerotic rim
- Histology: spindle cells in storiform pattern
- Usually resolve spontaneously

8.2.3 Osteoid osteoma
- Mechanism of pain: PGE2 & cyclooxygenase (COX1 & 2) →
  NSAIDs is first line of treatment
    - Refractory to NSAIDs → radiofrequency ablation
- Painful scoliosis due to paraspinal spasm: osteoid osteoma locates on
  concave side of apex of curve
    - Posterior elements of spine: osteoid osteoma, osteoblastoma &
      ABC

- Imaging (CT is best): central radiolucent nidus with surrounding reactive sclerotic bone
- Histology: woven (osteoid) bone, osteoblastic rimming
- Osteoblastoma: osteoid osteoma >1.5cm or 2cm in size is osteoblastoma
  - More locally aggressive & less responsive to NSAIDs than osteoid osteoma
- New non-invasive option (especially in anterior tibia) is MR-guided *high-intensity focused US (MR-HIFU)*

8.2.4 Osteochondroma
- Imaging: exostosis grows *away* from physis; medullary cavity of exostosis is continuous with medullary canal of involved bone
- Cartilage cap (hyaline cartilage) >2cm poses risk for malignant transformation
- Symptomatic osteochondroma that fails nonoperative treatment: marginal resection at base of stalk; make sure to remove entire cartilage cap
- Multiple hereditary exostoses (MHE)
  - Autosomal dominant: *EXT1* (most severe), EXT2, EXT3
    - EXT is important in synthesis of *heparan sulfate.*
    - 50% transmission rate (AD), 96% penetrance in females, 100% penetrance in males
      - Possible for 5% of siblings to have genetic mutation but not clinical manifestations
  - EXT1/2 are tumor suppressor genes → when *inactivated*, multiple exostoses result
  - MHE has 10% risk of malignant transformation to chondrosarcoma (compared to 1% risk with solitary osteochondroma).
    - Cartilage cap growth should cease after skeletal maturity
    - Adult cartilage cap thickness *>1cm* is concerning for chondrosarcoma.
  - MHE: short, LLD, long bone deformities, subluxation of radiocapitellar joints
    - MHE patient with loss of forearm rotation: marginal resection of osteochondroma to improve rotation

8.2.5 Eosinophilic granuloma
- Spine: vertebra plana
- Histology: Langerhan's cells with coffee bean nuclei, Birbeck granules
- Hand-Schuller-Christian: lytic skull lesions, diabetes insipidus, exophthalmos

8.2.6 Giant cell tumor
- Chest xray or CT to evaluate for lung metastasis
- Most common in distal femur
- Neoplastic cells are mononuclear stromal cells (*preosteoblastic mononuclear cells*), not multinucleated giant cells
- Treatment: denosumab (RANKL inhibitor); curettage & bone graft or cement
  - Adjuvant: argon beam, liquid nitrogen, phenol, hydrogen peroxide, denosumab

8.2.7 Unicameral bone cyst
- Central lytic lesion most commonly in metaphysis of proximal humerus
- Gets smaller & may spontaneously resolve with time
- Nonoperative unless symptomatic or impending fracture: curettage & bone grafting; or steroid injection
  - Pathologic fracture: "fallen leaf"
    - Nonoperative management of fracture (except proximal femoral pathologic fracture → ORIF with bone graft)

8.2.8 Aneurysmal bone cyst
- Ubiquitin-specific protease-6 (USP-6) link (this and nodular fasciitis)
- Recurrence risk associated w/ young age, open physes, incomplete initial curettage, higher Enneking staging, and periarticular location
- Compared to UBC, ABC is eccentric & expands greater than width of physis with multiple septae separating blood-filled cavities
- MRI shows "fluid-fluid levels", which correlate with "lakes of blood" on histology
- Curettage & bone graft

8.2.9 Bone tumors in anterior tibia

- Adamantinoma
    - Histology: nests of cells in palisading pattern
    - Metastasis to lungs
    - Wide excision
- Osteofibrous dysplasia (ossifying fibroma): osteoblastic rimming

8.2.10 Osteosarcoma
- Low grade and parosteal osteosarcomas (as well as ALTs) associated w/ MDM2
- C-FOS (tumor proto-oncogene) implicated in osteosarcoma
- Workup: xrays of entire extremity, MRI of entire extremity, whole body bone scan, CT chest, biopsy
    - Ewing sarcoma workup also includes bone marrow biopsy
    - Metastasis to lungs >>> bones
- Risk factors: Paget's, retinoblastoma (Rb), p53
- Generally presents as Enneking stage IIB (high-grade, extracompartmental)
- MSTS (Enneking) Staging System
    - Presence of mets at time of dx is worst prognostic indicator

Stage	Grade	Site	Metastasis
IA	Low	Intra	--
IB	Low	Extra	--
IIA	High	Intra	--
IIB	High	Extra	--
III	--	--	Yes

- Neoadjuvant chemotherapy for 8-12 weeks → wide surgical resection → adjuvant chemotherapy for 6-12 months
    - Improved overall survival if adjuvant chemotherapy is resumed within *18-21* days after surgery
    - 98% histologic tumor necrosis after neoadjuvant chemotherapy is good prognostic indicator.
        - Other: normal LDH at presentation
        - Worse prognosis if axial tumor or >10cm
    - Standard 3-drug treatment is *doxorubicin, cisplatin, and high-dose MTX*
- Local recurrence of primary malignant bone tumors is related to

surgical margin

Subtype	Imaging	
Intramedullary	Sunburst, Codman's triangle, metaphysis	Most common subtype (also called conventional)
Parosteal	Surface/juxtacortical of metaphysis ("stuck-on"), posterior cortex of distal femur	Wide excision only (no chemo) since low grade
Periosteal	Sunburst, Codman's triangle, diaphysis	
Telangiectatic	Eccentric lytic lesion	Lakes of blood; like ABC but with more malignant features

8.2.11 Ewing sarcoma
- Chemotherapy-surgery-chemotherapy
  - o Radiotherapy & chemotherapy (without surgery) can also be definitive treatment
- CD99+
- Tumor activation of Factor X to Xa is responsible for increased VTE risk in Ewing's
- Elevated LDH is associated with worse tumor burden
- Proximal femoral replacement for osteosarcoma or Ewing sarcoma: most common functional deficit is *abductor* weakness
- Distal femur ES or OS: most durable reconstruction is *rotationplasty*

8.2.12 Malignant fibrous histiocytoma (undifferentiated pleomorphic sarcoma)
- Malignant bone tumor that is similar to osteosarcoma in clinical presentation & on imaging
  - o Histology: pleomorphic spindle cells in storiform pattern
    - Unlike osteosarcoma, there is no osteoid formation
- Secondary MFH/UPS may arise from chronic bone infarct, Paget's or post-radiation
- Chemotherapy-surgery-chemotherapy

8.2.13 Multiple myeloma
- Plasma cells: clock-face, eccentric nucleus
    - SPEP (M spike): IgG >>> IgA heavy chains
    - UPEP: kappa or lambda light chains (Bence Jones proteins)
- CRAB: hypercalcemia, renal insufficiency, anemia, bone lesions
- Solitary lesion is plasmacytoma
- RANKL is responsible for punched-out lytic lesions
- Cold on bone scan: MM & thyroid carcinoma
- Treatment for MM: chemotherapy, bisphosphonates
    - Pathologic fracture: surgical stabilization, radiation & bisphosphonates
- Solitary lesion is plasmacytoma
    - Treatment of solitary plasmacytoma: radiation

8.2.14 Lymphoma
- B symptoms
- Diffuse lytic lesions, mottled, permeative
- Flow cytometry & cytogenetic analysis for diagnosis: need *unfixed* fresh tissue during biopsy
    - Histology: small round blue cells, CD20+, CD45+
- Chemotherapy +/- XRT

8.3 CARTILAGE TUMORS

8.3.1 Enchondroma
- Benign cartilage tumor in medullary cavity (popcorn stippling on radiographs)
    - Most common bone tumor in hand
- Hyperintense on T2 MR, isointense on T1
- Histology: hyaline cartilage (uniform chondrocytes in lacunae)
- Observation, radiographic surveillance
    - Symptomatic, unresponsive to nonoperative management: intralesional curettage & bone graft
- Isolated enchondroma: 1% risk of malignant transformation to chondrosarcoma.

- o Asymptomatic: obs; symptomatic: curettage and bone grafting (if in hand and associated fx fix accordingly)
- Ollier's disease: multiple enchondromas
  - o 30% risk of malignant transformation
- Maffucci's syndrome: multiple enchondromas, angiomas/hemangiomas, visceral malignancies
  - o 30% malignant transformation to chondrosarcoma, but 100% lifetime risk of developing a malignancy (chondrosarcoma, GI cancer, astrocytoma, etc.)
- Chondrosarcoma: cortical destruction, endosteal scalloping, periosteal reaction;
  - o Isolated enchondroma w/ 1% risk of transformation to solitary chondrosarcoma

8.3.2 Chondroblastoma
- Epiphyseal tumors: chondroblastoma, GCT, clear cell chondrosarcoma
- Xrays: lytic lesion in epiphysis that may cross physis, thin sclerotic rim
- Histology: "chicken wire" or "cobblestone" arrangement of chondroblasts
- Like GCT, can metastasize to lungs (obtain chest imaging)
- Symptomatic: curettage & bone graft

8.3.3 Periosteal chondroma
- Benign cartilage tumor on surface (juxtacortical) of long bones, most often in proximal humerus
- Imaging: stippled calcification, scalloping of cortex
- Observation if asymptomatic; marginal excision if symptomatic

8.3.4 Chondrosarcoma
- Recurrence is correlated with increased telomerase activity
- Clear cell chondrosarcoma: epiphyseal tumor
- Mesenchymal chondrosarcoma: responsive to *chemotherapy*
- Dedifferentiated chondrosarcoma: most aggressive; bimorphic (low-grade chondroid tumor & high-grade sarcoma)
- Wide surgical excision; chondrosarcoma generally does not respond to chemoradiation (except mesenchymal chondrosarcoma)

8.4 NERVE & NERVE SHEATH TUMORS

8.4.1 Schwannoma (neurilemmoma)
- Benign, associated with *neurofibromatosis II*
- Target sign on MRI
- Histology: S100+, Antoni A (hypercellular) & Antoni B (hypocellular) biphasic pattern
- Asymptomatic → observation; symptomatic → marginal resection

8.4.2 Malignant peripheral nerve sheath tumor (neurofibrosarcoma)
- Arise from peripheral nerve of neurofibroma (NF-1) → increased PET-CT uptake suggests malignant transformation
- S100+
- Wide excision & radiation

8.4.3 Neuroblastoma
- Most common solid tumor in children <2 years
- Usually in adrenal gland
- Small round blue cells arrange in rosette pattern

8.5 SOFT TISSUE TUMORS

8.5.1 Giant-cell tumor of tendon sheath
- Benign tumor of tendon sheath of hands & feet, analogous to PVNS
    - Hemosiderin
- PVNS & GCTTS: overexpression of colony stimulating factor 1 (*CSF-1*)
- "Localized tenosynovial giant cell" or "nodular synovitis"
- Peak age of occurrence 30-50yo, females > males
- Present as small painless nodules & 20% can have erosion into bone
- MRI: hypointense T1, hyperintense T2, diffuse enhancement w/ contrast
- Treatment: marginal excision; if recurrence (low): re-excision
    - High local recurrence after marginal excision

8.5.2 Desmoid tumor (extraabdominal fibromatosis)
- Common in paraspinal region & posterior distal femur (popliteal fossa)
- Associated with Gardner syndrome & familial adenomatous polyposis (FAP)
  - May consider colonoscopy
  - Elevated *β-catenin*, estrogen receptor β positive
- Treatment: estrogen receptor blocker (tamoxifen), wide resection & radiation

8.5.3 Lipoma
- Bright T1, dark on T2 & STIR MRI
- No need for biopsy only if 100% confident it's a lipoma on MRI
- Observation if asymptomatic; marginal resection if symptomatic

8.5.4 Soft tissue sarcoma
- Workup of a soft tissue mass: CT C/A/P, MRI of entire extremity, biopsy
  - Biopsy every soft tissue mass before surgery unless 100% confident it's a lipoma based on MRI
- Treatment is generally wide excision & radiotherapy
  - RT is especially important if margins are negative but not wide
- Unplanned excision with inadequate (positive) margins → MRI of entire extremity, CT C/A/P to exclude metastasis, then wide re-resection of surgical bed +/- radiation

8.5.5 Synovial sarcoma
- Origin is not synovium
- Most common malignant sarcoma of foot
- Biphasic: spindle cells & epithelial cells
- Vimentin+, epithelial membrane antigen

8.5.6 Liposarcoma
- Lipoblast (signet ring cell)
- Myxoid liposarcoma: retroperitoneal metastasis, therefore need CT C/A/P.
  - Good local control w/ radiation & surgery

  o   Retroperitoneal, soft-tissue, and bony mets
- Well-differentiated liposarcoma (atypical lipomatous tumor): marginal resection
- Other liposarcoma types: wide resection & radiation

8.5.7 Epithelioid sarcoma
- Most common soft tissue sarcoma of hand → can cause overlying skin ulceration (often mistaken for non-healing ulcer)
- Histology: keratin+

8.5.8 Leiomyosarcoma
- Malignant sarcoma of smooth muscle, *bone* leiomyosarcoma (lytic bone lesions with soft tissue extension)
- Spindle cells arrange in fascicles: actin, vimentin

8.5.9 Angiosarcoma
- Risk factor: polyvinyl chloride exposure
- CD31+

8.6 METASTATIC DISEASE

8.6.1 Basics
- Bone metastasis: breast, lung, thyroid, renal, phosphate
  o   Metastatic lung is worst prognosis, metastatic thyroid is best
  o   Spine is most common site of bone metastases via Batson's vertebral plexus
    ▪ Lytic lesion (lung, thyroid, renal, breast): RANKL
    ▪ Blastic lesion (prostate, breast): endothelin-1
    ▪ Metastatic spine lesion: spinal decompression & stabilization if neurologic deficits with life expectancy >6 months
  o   Metastatic lesions distal to elbows or knees are from lung >>> renal carcinoma
- If biopsy-proven isolated metastatic bony lesion: definitive treatment (resection & reconstruction)
- If multiple widespread lesions: chemotherapy, radiation therapy,

bisphosphonates and prophylactic fixation as needed
- o Embolization of renal carcinoma prior to surgery
- Proteinases divided into cathepsins (B and D) and MMPs (collagenase, stromelysin, gelatinase)
  - o Cathepsins: acid-activated hydrolyses that degrade collagen and essential in osteoclast-mediated bone resorption
  - o MMPs: family of Zn-binding enzymes that degrade ECM and vital in *cancer cell invasion of basement membranes, metastasis*

8.6.2 Lymphatic metastasis
- SCARE: synovial cell, clear cell, angiosarcoma, rhabdomyosarcoma, epithelioid
  - o Rhabdomyosarcoma: most common sarcoma in children

8.6.3 Prophylactic fixation
- History of primary cancer with new isolated bone lesion or multiple bone lesions: metastatic workup (including CT C/A/P) & biopsy before surgery
- If pathologic fracture with no clear diagnosis (even if it's a femoral shaft fracture), perform biopsy & splint before surgery
- If IMN is performed & biopsy returns as primary bone sarcoma (e.g., chondrosarcoma) without evidence of metastasis, the entire bone is now contaminated; definitive treatment requires wide resection, which may involve amputation
- Recommend surgery if Mirel's score >8

Score	1	2	3
Site	Upper limb	Lower limb	Peritrochanteric
Pain	Mild	Moderate	Functional
Lesion	Blastic	Mixed	Lytic
Size	<1/3	1/3 – 2/3	>2/3

- Prophylactic fixation with load sharing device plus radiation
  - o Single radiation (vs multifraction): equivalent pain relief, lower cost

8.7 OTHERS

8.7.1 Myositis ossificans
- Fibrodysplasia ossificans progressiva (FOP, stone man disease): diffuse, progressive HO; mutation of activin A type I receptor (ACVR1), which is a BMP receptor
- Myositis ossificans: peripheral ossification, central lucency
  - Compared to malignancy, which generally has central ossification
- Wait until maturation (cold on bone scan) before resection.

8.7.2 Melorheostosis
- Dysplasia of cortical bone → hyperostosis, flowing candle wax along cortical surface.
- Treatment is obs & medical treatment of symptoms

8.7.3 Pigmented villonodular synovitis (PVNS)
- Overexpression of Colony-stimulating factor-1 (CSF-1)
- Hemosiderin deposits → low signal on T1 & T2 MRI
- "tenosynovial giant cell tumor"
- Symptomatic → marginal excision (synovectomy) +/- radiation

8.7.4 Synovial chondromatosis
- Intraarticular loose bodies comprising synovium / cartilage
- Symptomatic → synovectomy & removal of loose bodies
- Histology: synovial metaplasia

8.7.5 Dermatofibrosarcoma protuberans
- Increased PDGF-beta
- Cutaneous soft tissue sarcoma

8.7.6 Glomus tumor
- Subungual bluish lesion: paroxysmal pain, cold intolerance
- Small round blue cells
- Marginal excision

8.7.7 Chordoma

- Malignant tumor of notochodral cells, most common in sacrum/coccyx
- Histology: physaliferous cells, keratin+, S100+
- Wide resection (vertebrectomy with anterior & posterior reconstruction) +/- radiation

8.7.8 Hemangioma / vascular malformation
- Phlebolith on xrays; MRI → heterogeneous mass ("bag of worms")
- Chronic mass that changes in size with activity
- Asymptomatic → observation; symptomatic → sclerotherapy, embolization or resection

8.7.9 Tumoral calcinosis
- Dysfunction of phosphate regulation → periarticular calcinosis in extra-capsular soft tissues
    - More prevalent in African-Americans
    - Mutations in *FGF23*

8.7.10 Fibrodysplasia ossificans progressive (FOP)
- Autosomal dominant; defect in ACVR1 gene, which codes a type 1 BMP receptor, results in constitutive activation and transduction via SMAD and MAPK signaling pathways
- Involves replacement of all connective tissue w/ bone, ankylosis of joints; surgery contraindicated because can make it worse

DOMAIN 9: PEDIATRICS

9.1 BASICS

9.1.1 Elbow ossification centers
- Age at ossification (CRITOE): capitellum (1), radial head (3), internal/medial epicondyle (5), trochlea (7), olecranon (9), external/lateral epicondyle (11)
- Medial epicondyle is last to fuse
- Growth rate of upper extremity: proximal humerus 80%, distal humerus 20%

9.1.2 Nonaccidental trauma
- Skin lesion is most common finding, followed by fracture
- Femur fracture in nonambulatory infant (<3 years); *metaphyseal* corner fracture; posterior rib fracture; multiple fractures in different stages of healing
  - Transphyseal separation of distal humerus (usually posteromedial displacement) → child abuse: radiocapitellar line is preserved; CRPP
  - Elbow dislocation: radiocapitellar line is disrupted
  - May require arthrogram to differentiate the two
- Transverse is femur fracture pattern most commonly associated with abuse
- Child abuse is second (after accidental injury) most common cause of death in children

9.1.3 Leg length discrepancy
- Greatest skeletal linear growth occurs during first year of life
- If there is contracture across any joint, *CT scanography* provides best measurement of LLD
- Menelaus method: girl reaches skeletal maturity at 14 years, boys at 16 years
  - Proximal femur: 3 mm/yr
  - Distal femur: 9 mm/yr

- o Proximal tibia: 6 mm/yr
- o Distal tibia: 5 mm/yr
- Projected LLD at skeletal maturity:
  - o <2cm: nonoperative (shoe lift)
  - o 2-5cm: epiphysiodesis
  - o >5cm: limb lengthening
- Lower extremity deformity
  - o In general, varus deformity is corrected at the proximal tibia while valgus deformity is corrected at the distal femur
  - o Dome osteotomy provides the most bone contact with the least amount of translation & shortening

9.1.4 Physeal arrest
- Partial arrest results in angular deformity; complete arrest results in limb length discrepancy
- If physeal bar <50% of physis & kid has >2 years or 2cm of growth remaining: bar resection & interposition (such as with PMMA)
  - o Otherwise, complete epiphysiodesis & address limb length discrepancy if needed

9.1.5 Cerebral palsy
- *Static* encephalopathy, onset before *2 years* old
- Baclofen to treat spasticity: activates GABA receptors → inhibits action potentials
- Sitting at age 2 is best predictor for ability to ambulate
- Voluntary control of motion is best predictor of functional improvement after surgery for upper extremity deformity
- Neuromuscular hip dysplasia: acetabular deficiency is *posterosuperior*; migration index (severity of dysplasia) correlates with GMFCS level
  - o <4 years old: adductor & psoas release
  - o >4 years old:
    - ▪ Functioning child: Dega osteotomy & proximal femoral osteotomy
    - ▪ Non-functioning (GMFCS V): femoral head resection & proximal femoral osteotomy

9.1.6 Lyme

- Borrelia burgdorferi transmission via deer tick (Ixodes)
- Erythema migrans, CN7 palsy, carditis, encephalopathy
- If no neurologic or cardiac symptoms: doxycycline (not in children <8 years) or amoxicillin for 28 days
  - If neurologic or cardiac symptoms: IV ceftriaxone, cefotaxime or PCN G
- No need for surgical lavage for Lyme arthritis

9.1.7 Miscellaneous
- Congenital upper extremity amputation: prosthesis fitting at 6 months (sitting age)
- Congenital lower extremity amputation: prosthesis fitting at 12 months (walking age)
- Rett syndrome: ataxia, hypotonia, chorea, NM scoliosis
  - X-linked dominant: male fetuses usually die in utero
- Pedi pelvic fx: if triradiate cartilage is open, iliac wing is weaker than elastic pelvic ligaments, resulting in bone failure before pelvic ring disruption
  - Usually treated non-op, but if displacement >2cm or if vertical or rotatory instability are present then surgical treatment indicated
- Amniotic constriction band syndrome (ABS) associated w/ clubfoot, cleft palate, and acrosyndactyly
  - 3 theories: 1) germ plasm developmental abnormality resulting in constriction rings (possibly secondar to vascular disruption), 2) intrauterine disruption, 3) intrauterine trauma
- 7% or greater cross-sectional area (CSA) violation of physis w/out implant placement portends high risk of growth arrest (Makela et al)
  - *With implant placement* (Knapik et al): 8% violation w/ growth arrest; 3-7% or less w/ metallic implant probably tolerable

9.2 UPPER EXTREMITY TRAUMA

9.2.1 Radial neck fracture
- <30° angulation: cast without reduction

- >30° angulation: closed reduction & casting
  - If failed closed reduction (persistent angulation >30°) →
    percutaneous vs open reduction +/- pinning

9.2.2 Nursemaid's elbow
- Radial head subluxation with interposition of annular ligament in
  radiocapitellar joint
- Reduction by supinating & flexing elbow; no need for immobilization
  post-reduction

9.2.3 Pediatric distal radius fracture
- Short arm cast
- Cast index (sagittal width / coronal width) >0.8 is predictor of fracture
  re-displacement in cast

9.2.4 Pediatric both bone forearm fracture (BBFF)
- Assess rotation: AP xray (radial styloid & biceps tuberosity should be
  180°), lateral xray (ulnar styloid & coronoid should be 180°)
- Distal third BBFF: *short* arm cast; more proximal BBFF requires
  long arm cast
- Reduction & immobilization with thumb pointing *away* from apex of
  fracture
  - Apex volar (supination injury): pronates forearm
  - Apex dorsal (pronation injury): supinates forearm

9.2.5 Supracondylar humerus fracture
- Initial treatment for Gartland type II-IV SCH is CRPP regardless of
  vascular status
  - Pink, pulseless hand: after CRPP, if the hand is pink & perfused
    but pulseless → maintain fixation & observation in hospital
    overnight
    - Pink, pulseless hand (normal capillary refill, absent
      radial pulse) is usually due to brachial artery spasm
    - After CRPP, if hand is not pink & perfused → remove
      pins, unreduce fracture & assess perfusion; if still not
      perfused → exploration of antecubital fossa

- - Under perfused, pulseless hand: after CRPP, if hand remains under perfused → exploration
- Standard of care: 2 or 3 lateral pins
  - Medial pin: ulnar nerve neurapraxia due to "tenting" of nerve over pin
    - Higher risk of ulnar nerve injury if medial pin is placed with elbow flexed, which brings ulnar nerve anteriorly over medial epicondyle
  - Crossed pins are biomechanically more stable
  - Extension-type: CRPP with elbow in flexion
  - Flexion-type: CRPP with elbow in extension
- Pin removal at 3 weeks
- Younger age is risk factor for pin site infection (<4.4yo)
- SCH fracture with ipsilateral BBFF: higher nerve palsy & compartment syndrome
- Neurapraxia: extension-type (AIN >>> radial), flexion-type (ulnar)
  - Treatment: observation
- Interposition blocking reduction: extension-type (brachialis, median nerve, brachial artery), flexion-type (ulnar nerve)
- PT after CRPP of SCH fracture does not affect functional or motion recovery

9.2.6 Lateral condyle fracture
- Internal oblique view is best to evaluate fracture displacement
- CRPP if >2mm displacement; open reduction & pinning if unable to obtain anatomic reduction
  - Vascular supply comes posteriorly → avoid posterior dissection to prevent lateral condyle AVN
- Cubitus valgus: tardy ulnar nerve palsy; supracondylar osteotomy if needed
- Lateral spurring (overgrowth) is minimized by anatomic reduction of lateral condyle fracture
- LCL is usually intact & attached to lateral condyle fragment proximally & radial neck distally

9.2.7 Medial humeral epicondyle fracture

- Best view to determine displacement: distal humerus axial view.
- Should get arthrogram or MRI to evaluate degree of displacement if concerning on XR

9.3 UPPER EXTREMITY DEFORMITY

9.3.1 Trigger finger
- Pediatric trigger thumb: Notta's node (thickened flexor tendon nodule)
  o Fixed deformity >1 year of age: release A1 pulley
  o Be careful of *radial* digital nerve crossing surgical field
- Pediatric trigger finger
  o In addition to A1 pulley release, may need to release one or both FDS slips

9.3.2 Obstetric brachial plexus birth palsy (OBPBP)
- Most common is upper trunk injury (Erb's palsy, C5-6): better prognosis because of preserved hand function
- Parents should perform passive stretching with emphasis on shoulder elevation/abduction & ER
- Ability to flex elbow (biceps) by 3 months is best predictor of complete recovery of OBPBP
- Elbow flexion contracture: most effective initial treatment is serial casting
- Late presentation: internal rotation contracture, posterior glenohumeral dysplasia & dislocation
  o >5 years old: proximal humerus derotation osteotomy to improve external rotation

9.3.3 Sprengel deformity
- Like Poland syndrome, thought to be due to embryonic vascular interruption
- Associated with omovertebral body, Klippel-Feil syndrome, congenital scoliosis
- Shoulder abduction is most limited

9.4 LOWER EXTREMITY TRAUMA

9.4.1 Pelvic avulsion fracture
- Treatment: unless patient is an elite athlete → symptom management, activity restriction, progression to WBAT
  - Relative indication for surgery: displacement >2 cm
- Iliac crest contusion (hip pointer): direct trauma, no fracture

Apophyseal avulsion	Muscle(s)	Nerve
AIIS	Rectus femoris (direct head)	Femoral
ASIS	Sartorius	Femoral
Ischium	Hamstrings & adductors	Hamstrings (tibial), adductors (obturator)
Pubic symphysis	Abdominal muscles	
Iliac crest	Abdominal muscles	
Lesser trochanter	Iliopsoas	Psoas (lumbar plexus), iliacus (femoral)

9.4.2 Pediatric proximal femur fracture
- Injury to greater trochanter apophysis → coxa valga (>135°); overgrowth of apophysis → coxa vara (<120°)
- Most common complication is AVN (injury to MFCA)

9.4.3 Pediatric femoral shaft fracture
- <6 months: Pavlik harness
- 6 months to 5 years: spica cast
- 5-11 years:
  - Length stable: flexible nail
    - Estimating flexible nail size: (isthmic canal diameter x 0.8) / 2, which is same as taking isthmic canal diameter x 0.4
  - Length unstable: submuscular plate
- >11 years or >100 lbs: intramedullary nail or submuscular plate
  - Avoid piriformis entry IMN → injury to lateral epiphyseal vessels (deep branches of MFCA) leading to femoral head AVN

9.4.4 Pediatric distal femur fracture
- Growth rate: proximal femur 3 mm/yr, distal femur 9 mm/yr
- Smooth K-wires for *transphyseal* percutaneous fixation
- For fracture with large Thurston-Holland fragment, percutaneous screw fixation with screws parallel to physis
- Most common complication after surgery is *physeal arrest.*
- If significantly displaced, need to watch for vascular injury → ABI if needed. If so, stabilization and vascular repair w/in 6 hrs; low threshold for fasciotomies

9.4.5 Tibial eminence fracture
- Type I: nondisplaced → immobilize with knee in extension
- Type II: minimally displaced with intact posterior hinge → closed reduction, immobilize in extension
- Type III: completely displaced → open vs arthroscopic reduction internal fixation

9.4.6 Tibial tubercle avulsion fracture
- *Compartment syndrome* due to injury to anterior tibial recurrent artery
- Premature closure of tibial tubercle apophysis can lead to recurvatum deformity
- Loss of straight leg raise on exam

9.4.7 Proximal tibial metaphyseal fracture
- Genu valgum (Cozen's phenomenon): observation; valgus deformity usually spontaneously resolves but affected limb will be *longer*
  - Initial treatment of fracture in long leg cast with *varus mold* to minimize risk of valgus deformity

9.4.8 Pediatric ankle fracture
- Tillaux fracture (SH III): avulsion of AITFL (external rotation injury)
  - Obtain CT scan to evaluate step off
- Triplane fracture (SH IV): SH II in lateral view & SH III in AP view
  - Obtain CT scan
- Distal tibial physis: central physis is first to close, while anterolateral physis is last → transitional fractures (Tillaux, triplane) often affect

anterolateral physis
  - o Long leg cast immobilization: articular step off <2mm
    - Internally rotate foot to reduce fracture
  - o >2mm step off: CRPP vs ORIF
- SHII distal tibia fracture: entrapment of torn anterior *periosteum* may prevent successful closed reduction
  - o External foot/ankle rotation deformity is more common than internal
- Cast with ankle between neutral to resting plantarflexion (37°) to decrease risk for compartment syndrome

9.5 LOWER EXTREMITY DEFORMITY

9.5.1 Developmental dysplasia of hip (DDH)
- Risk factors: firstborn, female, breech, family history
- Barlow's exam dislocates hip, Ortolani's exam relocates it
- Acetabular deficiency is *anterolateral* (compared to neuromuscular hip dysplasia, which is *posterosuperior*)
- US before 4-6 months, xrays after 4-6 months when ossific nucleus is visible
- Xrays: Perkin & Hilgenreiner lines → ossific nucleus should be in inferomedial quadrant
- Alpha angle (normally >60°) on US determines degree of horizontalization of acetabular sourcil
- Beta angle (normally <55°) measures displacement of hip abductor muscles
- Treatment
  - o <6 months: Pavlik harness
    - Pavlik harness only if hip is relocatable
    - If hip is still dislocated after 3 weeks of full-time harness, switch to semirigid abduction orthosis
    - If still dislocated with semirigid abduction orthosis → closed vs open reduction, spica casting
    - Hyperflexion in harness → femoral nerve palsy (loss of limb kicking)
      - Discontinue harness completely & observe for

return of function
- Hyper-abduction in harness → impingement of posterosuperior retinacular branch of MFCA leading to AVN
  - o 6-18 months: closed reduction & spica casting
    - Block to reduction: inverted labrum, inverted limbus, transverse acetabular ligament, capsule, pulvinar, ligamentum teres
  - o >18 months: open reduction +/- osteotomy & spica casting
    - DDH is associated with femoral anteversion & coxa valga: VDRO
    - Open approach is usually anterior (Smith-Peterson) to minimize risk to MFCA
- Residual acetabular dysplasia, open triradiate: *Pemberton* osteotomy
  - o Can also do Salter osteotomy
- Residual acetabular dysplasia, closed triradiate: periacetabular osteotomy (PAO)
- Adult hip dysplasia: lateral center edge angle <20°, Tonnis angle >10°

9.5.2 Legg-Calve-Perthes (coxa plana)
- Young children: activity modification & symptomatic treatment
  - o Age <6 years is best prognostic factor
- Containment-type surgery (femoral +/- pelvic osteotomy) for AVN is for older children between 8-11 years
- Core decompression is for adults
- Bilateral, symmetrical involvement → multiple epiphyseal dysplasia (MED)

9.5.3 Congenital knee dislocation / hyperextension
- If knee can be passively flexed to neutral: manipulation with serial casting, followed by bracing
  - o Done at bedside to avoid anesthesia
- If knee cannot be flexed to neutral: open reduction (quadriceps lengthening, soft tissue release)
- Associated with myelomeningocele, arthrogryposis, DDH, clubfoot

o   If hip & knee are both dislocated, treat knee first

9.5.4 Congenital longitudinal deficiency

- Includes proximal femoral focal deficiency, fibular hemimelia, ACL deficiency, tarsal coalition
- Sonic hedge-hog (SHH) gene regulates limb bud formation
- Fibular hemimelia: absent lateral rays, equinovalgus foot
    o   Functional, plantigrade foot: surgery to address LLD
    o   Nonfunctional, non-plantigrade foot: syme amputation

9.5.5 Slipped capital femoral epiphysis (SCFE)

- Metaphysis slips anterior & superior relative to epiphysis
    o   MRI shows metaphyseal edema
- Slip is through *hypertrophic zone* of growth plate
- Obligator external rotation with hip flexion; referred knee pain because of medial obturator nerve
- Risk factors: obesity & endocrinopathy (especially hypothyroidism)
- AVN is highest risk in unstable SCFE (unable to bear weight)
- Acute if symptomatic for <3 weeks, chronic if >3 weeks
- In situ fusion (*single* cannulated screw): starting point should be proximal & anterior (compared to CRPP for adult hip fracture)
    o   Screw should be lateral to intertrochanteric line to prevent screw impingement with acetabulum/labrum during hip flexion
    o   Consider prophylactic fixation of contralateral hip if <10 years old or has endocrine disorder
- Obese w/ SCFE vs obese controls: obese w/ SCFE had *increased leptin* and *increased rates of hypertension*

9.5.6 Genu valgum

- Max physiologic genu valgum occurs between age 2-4 years
- Consider *distal femoral medial* plate hemiepiphysiodesis if >7 years old with valgus >12°
    o   Hueter-Volkmann principle: compression across growth plate slows growth
- Large deformity with inadequate growth remaining for hemiepiphysiodesis: distal femoral varus osteotomy

9.5.7 Tibial bowing
- Posteromedial: physiologic, observation
    - o May have limb length discrepancy at skeletal maturity
    - o Associated with calcaneovalgus foot deformity
- Anterolateral: NF I
    - o Bowing without fracture or pseudarthrosis: total contact orthosis
    - o Bowing with acute fracture: long leg cast is initial treatment of choice
    - o Pseudarthrosis: surgical fixation (usually intramedullary device) with bone graft
- Anteromedial: fibular hemimelia

9.5.8 Blount's disease
- Normal
    - o Physiologic genu varum until <2 years old → maximum genu valgum at 3 years old → physiologic genu valgum at 7 years old
- Infantile Blount's disease (tibia vara): kids 2-5 years old
    - o Mild disease (stage I & II) in kids <3 years-old: valgus-inducing KAFO brace (unload medial compartment)
    - o Moderate to severe disease (stage III-VI), or kids >3 years old: proximal tibia/fibula valgus osteotomy
        - ▪ Overcorrect 10-15° valgus
- Adolescent Blount's: >10 years old, usually unilateral
    - o Small deformity with adequate growth remaining to correct deformity: lateral tibia/fibula hemiepiphysiodesis
    - o Large deformity, skeletally mature: proximal tibia/fibula osteotomy

9.5.9 Congenital vertical talus
- Rigid rocker bottom / flatfoot deformity due to dorsal dislocation of navicular on talus
- Plantarflexion lateral xray
    - o Oblique talus: talonavicular joint is reduced
    - o CVT: persistent dorsal dislocation of navicular
        - ▪ Meary angle >20°: angle between longitudinal axis of talus & longitudinal axis of 1st MT

- Reverse Ponseti serial casting followed by surgery at 6-12 months of age (soft tissue releases, reduction of TN joint & pinning)
  - Refractory cases → talectomy; triple arthrodesis

9.5.10 Rotational deformity of lower extremity
- *Foot* progression angle determines in-toeing (negative value) or out-toeing (positive value)
- Three common causes of in-toeing
  - Metatarsus adductus (infant)
  - Internal tibial torsion (toddler)
    - Thigh foot progression angle determines tibial torsion
      - Internal tibial torsion: internal thigh foot progression angle (negative value)
      - External tibial torsion: external thigh foot progression angle (positive value)
  - Femoral anteversion (childhood): associated with packaging disorders (e.g., DDH, metatarsus adductus, congenital muscular torticollis)
    - Increased hip IR
- Two common causes of out-toeing
  - External rotation contracture of hips
  - External tibial torsion

9.5.11 Talipes equinovarus (clubfoot)
- Order of correction with Ponseti casting → CAVE: midfoot cavus, forefoot adductus, hindfoot varus & equinus
  - Ponseti casting → tendo-Achilles lengthening (TAL) with final cast → foot abduction orthosis
  - Treatment for recurrence after Ponseti casting (most often due to noncompliance with postsurgical bracing) is *recasting*
- Extensive soft tissue release is associated with poor long-term foot function
- Dynamic supination following Ponseti casting: anterior tibialis transfer to lateral cuneiform
- Dorsal bunion following Ponseti casting (dorsiflexed first MT): FHL lengthening & FHB flexor to extensor transfer

9.5.12 Charcot Marie Tooth disease (CMTD)
- *Autosomal dominant* is most common form, duplication of peripheral myelin protein 22 (*PMP22*) on chromosome 17
- Cavovarus foot, claw toes/hammertoes
- Intrinsic foot muscles (longest axons) are first to be weakened

9.6 CONGENITAL CONDITIONS

9.6.1 Osteogenesis imperfecta
- Autosomal dominant & recessive forms, COL1A1/COL1A2 → *missense* mutation resulting in substitution of glycine (GLY) for another amino acid in procollagen → impaired cross-linking of collagen
- Congenital anterolateral radial head dislocations, olecranon avulsion fracture, basilar invagination → myelopathy
- Blue sclera, dentinogenesis imperfecta
- Bisphosphonates: long-term use will show parallel metaphyseal bands on xrays
- Fix fractures with intramedullary (load-sharing) constructs

9.6.2 Achondroplasia
- Autosomal dominant, gain of function mutation of FGF3R → inhibits chondrocytes in *zone of proliferation*, thus impairing endochondral bone formation
- Risk factor: advanced paternal age
- Thoracolumbar kyphosis will likely resolve at walking age
- Lumbar spinal stenosis due to short pedicles & decreased interpedicular distance; normal intelligence; trident hands
- Stenosis of *foramen magnum* → central apnea
- Champagne glass pelvis, genu varum
- Rhizomelic dwarfism: disproportionate limbs (arms shorter than forearms, thighs shorter than legs)

9.6.3 Osteopetrosis
- Marble bone disease: osteoclast dysfunction
- Linked to defect in TCIRG1 gene, which encodes a subunit of the proton pump in osteoclast

- o Impaired osteoclast carbonic anhydrase activity → cannot acidify Howship lacunae for bone resorption.
  - o Dysregulated *osteoclast* activity
- Cranial nerve palsies (especially optic nerve), pancytopenia due to encroachment of bone marrow
- Erlenmeyer flask femur, rugger jersey spine

9.6.4 Neurofibromatosis
- Autosomal dominant, NF1 gene (neurofibromin)
- Smooth café-au-lait spots, optic glioma, axillary freckling, Lisch nodules (iris hamartomas), dystrophic scoliosis, hemihypertrophy, anterolateral bowing of tibia, pseudarthrosis of tibia/radius/ulna
- NF2: vestibular schwannomas
- Neurofibromas may transform into malignant peripheral nerve sheath tumors
  - o Malignant transformation is associated with increased uptake on PET-CT

9.6.5 Larsen syndrome
- Bilateral congenital hip, knee & elbow dislocations (specifically radial head dislocations); clubfoot; cervical kyphosis (need cervical spine imaging)
- Filamin B mutation

9.6.6 Friedreich's ataxia
- Autosomal recessive, GAA repeat mutation in *frataxin* gene → absent of frataxin leads to spinocerebellar degeneration (primarily posterior columns of spinal cord)
- Cavovarus foot, ataxia, areflexia, scoliosis

9.6.7 Marfan syndrome
- Autosomal dominant, fibrillin-1 (FBN1) gene
  - o Mutation prevents binding of TGF-b, thus increased levels of TGF-b in tissue which are associated w/ aortic dilatation
- Dolichostenomelia, arachnodactyly, scoliosis, protrusio acetabuli, dural ectasia, pectus excavatum, aortic root dilation, mitral valve prolapse,

superior lens dislocation

9.6.8 Muscular dystrophy
- X-lined recessive
  - o Duchenne: absent dystrophin
  - o Becker: decreased dystrophin
- XLR: mothers are carrier for gene and can pass to sons at rate of 50%
  - o Sons nearly always symptomatic if carry the gene
  - o Daughters also w/ 50% rate of carrying gene but nearly always *asymptomatic*
- Calf pseudohypertrophy (Gower's sign), elevated CPK
- Corticosteroid slows progression
- Scoliosis: early posterior spinal fusion (20-30° curve) to prevent restrictive lung disease

9.6.9 Multiple epiphyseal dysplasia (MED)
- Usually autosomal dominant; cartilage oligometric matrix protein (*COMP*) mutation → type II collagen dysfunction
- Impaired endochondral ossification of epiphyses
- Disproportionate dwarfism

9.6.10 Spondyloepiphyseal dysplasia (SED)
- COL2A1 mutation
- Autosomal dominant (SED congenita), X-linked recessive (SED tarda)
- Atlantoaxial instability → myelopathy

9.6.11 Diastrophic dysplasia
- Autosomal recessive, DTDST gene (sulfate transport protein)
- Rhizomelic dwarfism, cauliflower ears, hitchhiker's thumb, clubfeet, cervical kyphosis, cleft palate

9.6.12 Metaphyseal chondrodysplasia
- Metaphysis is dysplastic while epiphysis is normal
- Jansen: autosomal dominant, activating mutation of PTHrP leading to delayed maturation in zone of hypertrophy

9.6.13 Cleidocranial dysplasia

- Autosomal dominant, Runx2/Cbfa1 mutation → impaired intramembranous ossification
- Midline structures are affected: hypoplastic or absent clavicles, wide pubic symphysis, open fontanels

9.6.14 Campomelic dysplasia

- SOX9 mutation
- Bowing of long bones with overlying cutaneous dimpling, hypoplastic scapulae

9.6.15 Mucopolysaccharidosis (lysosomal storage disease)

- Proportionate dwarfism, carpal tunnel syndrome

Disease	Genetic	Enzyme	Accumulation	Unique features
Morquio	AR	Galactosamine-6-sulfate sulphatase, β-galactosidase	Keratan sulfate	Odontoid hypoplasia → atlantoaxial instability; normal intelligence
Hurler	AR	α-L iduronidase	Dermatan sulfate	--
San Filippo	AR	--	Heparan sulfate	--
Hunter	X-linked recessive	Sulpho-iduronate-sulphatase	Dermatan/heparan sulfate	Clear cornea

9.6.16 Down syndrome

- Advanced maternal age
- Trisomy 21: type 6 collagen leads to ligamentous laxity
- Atlantoaxial & occipitocervical instability, hip dysplasia due to hypotonia, patellofemoral instability

9.6.17 Beckwith-Wiedemann syndrome
- Hemihypertrophy, macroglossia, Wilm's tumor (requires frequent abdominal & pelvic ultrasounds, alpha-fetoprotein levels)

9.6.18 Ehler-Danlos syndrome
- COL5A1/COL5A2 mutation
- Echo to evaluate aortic root dilation
- Beighton-Horan scale to evaluate joint laxity

9.6.19 Gaucher disease
- Sphingolipid lyposomal storage disorder
- Autosomal recessive, β-glucocerebrosidase

9.7 SPINE

9.7.1 Torticollis
- Congenital muscular torticollis
  - Palpable mass (SCM), usually painless; associated with other congenital packaging deformity such as DDH
  - SCM contracture: head tilts *toward* while chin rotates *away* affected side
  - US of SCM shows fibrosis
  - Stretching of SCM is treatment of choice; SCM lengthening/release if fails nonoperative treatment
    - Stretch in direction opposite of contracture: tilt head *away* while rotate chin *toward* affected side
- Benign paroxysmal torticollis: episodic torticollis associated with pallor, agitation & ataxia
  - Typically resolves by age 3
- Klippel-Feil syndrome: short webbed neck, low hairline, limited neck ROM
  - Failure of segmentation or resegmentation of somites
  - Associated with congenital scoliosis & Sprengel deformity, block vertebrae—puts increased stress at C1-2 and prone to injury (contraindication to contact sports)

162

- Atlantoaxial rotatory subluxation

9.7.2 Atlantoaxial rotatory subluxation
- Painful torticollis
- Usually associated with URI (Grisel's disease), trauma or head/neck surgery
- Gold standard for diagnosis is dynamic CT
- <1 week: soft collar, NSAIDs
- >1 week: head halter traction, muscle relaxant → hard collar for 3 months
- Chronic (>4 weeks): halo traction → halo-vest immobilization for 3 months
- If above treatment fails or neurologic deficits → posterior C1-2 fusion
- Pseudosubluxation of cervical spine: usually C2 on C3; reduction with extension radiograph

9.7.3 Pediatric spondylolysis / spondylolisthesis
- Repetitive hyperextension → pars stress reaction
  - Acute, symptomatic: TLSO bracing
- Exam: loss of normal lumbar lordosis, tight hamstrings, pain with single-limb standing lumbar extension
- If xrays are normal, *SPECT* is most sensitive study to diagnose spondylolysis
- Most prevalent in *Native Americans*

9.7.4 Adolescent idiopathic scoliosis: 10-18 years old
- Most often *right* thoracic curve, female
- Risser stage 0 is highest risk of curve progression (peak growth velocity)
- Bracing if >25° curve in skeletally immature (girl <15 years, boy <16 years)
  - Wear for >12.9 hours per day
- Pedicle screw instrumentation: improve pullout strength by (1) tap 1mm smaller than screw diameter & (2) place screw via straightforward trajectory (vs anatomic trajectory)
- Smallest pedicles in T-spine: T4-6

- Smallest pedicle in L-spine: L1

9.7.5 Early onset scoliosis
- EOS affects kids <10 years old
  - Usually require MRI to rule out neural axis pathologies
- Infantile idiopathic scoliosis: ≤3 years old, male & *left* thoracic curve
  - Rib vertebral angle difference (RVAD) >20° is predictor of curve progression
    - Serial casting
- Juvenile idiopathic scoliosis: 4-10 years old
- Congenital scoliosis
  - VACTERL: remember to obtain renal US & echo
  - Congenital scoliosis secondary to hemivertebra: vertebral excision & short-segment instrumented fusion
  - Unilateral unsegmented bar with contralateral hemivertebra: greatest curve progression
  - Block vertebra: lowest curve progression
  - Unlike AIS, no hereditary basis or genetic link
- Neuromuscular scoliosis
  - Cerebral palsy, SMA, muscular dystrophy, spina bifida: surgery early (posterior instrumented spinal fusion)
  - Extend fusion caudally to include pelvis
- Of all pulmonary parameters, growing rods have effect on *forced vital capacity (FVC)* only

9.7.6 Myelodysplasia
- Folate deficiency, alpha fetoprotein (AFP)
- Myelomeningocele:
  - Fracture presents like infection / osteomyelitis: swelling, erythema, +/- elevated ESR/CRP
    - In patient with myelomeningocele, this is a fracture until proven otherwise
  - Latex hypersensitivity: type I hypersensitivity (IgE mediated)
- Neurocentral synchondrosis (NCS) closes first in cervical → lumbar → thoracic spine
- Caudal regression syndrome (sacral agenesis): maternal diabetes is risk factor

9.7.7 Spinal muscular atrophy (SMA)

- Also known as Werdnig-Hoffman disease
- Death of alpha motor neurons in anterior horn → progressive motor weakness (proximal to distal)
- Autosomal recessive: mutation of survival motor neuron 1 (SMN1) gene
    - Type I is more severe than type II
- Neuromuscular scoliosis & neuromuscular hip dislocation; tongue fasciculations & absent DTR

DOMAIN 10: BASIC SCIENCE

10.1 BASICS

10.1.1 Genetics & molecular biology

Test	Purpose
Southern blot	Detect DNA
Western blot	Detect protein
Northern blot	Detect RNA
siRNA	Block mRNA translation
RT-PCR	Convert RNA to DNA

- o Anticipation: future generation displays more severe form of disease & at an earlier age
  - o Examples: Huntington disease, myotonic dystrophy, Friedreich ataxia
- o Imprinting: gene expression (phenotype) occurs from only one allele (either from father's or mother's)
  - o Examples: Prader-Willi (paternal inheritance) & Angelman (maternal inheritance)
- o Epigenetics: inheritance by modifying gene expression rather than altering genetic code
  - o Examples: DNA methylation, histone acetylation / deacetylation

10.1.2 RANK/RANKL pathway
- Rheumatoid: T cells produce RANKL causing bone erosion
- Cancer cells produce RANKL → osteoclastogenesis; responsible for lytic lesions
- RANK/RANKL is responsible for osteolysis around orthopaedic implants
- RANKL is responsible for osteoclast differentiation from monocyte/macrophage lineage (hematopoietic)
  - o Osteoblasts are derived from mesenchymal stem cell lineage

10.1.3 Wnt/BMP pathway
- Sclerostin blocks pathway (inhibits osteoblastogenesis) → decreased bone formation

166

10.1.4 Gene expression

Gene expression	Lineage
PPARy2	Adipose
SOX9	Cartilage
Cbfa1/Runx2	Osteoblast

10.1.5 Important factors

Factor	Importance
TFG-β	Stimulate cartilage regeneration in vitro
Scleraxis	Tendon & ligament formation
IL-6	Osteolysis around implant

10.1.6 Vitamin D

- Sunlight helps synthesize Vit D3 (cholecalciferol) on skin surface → gets hydroxylated in liver to 25-(OH) Vit D3 [*25-hydroxyvitamin D3*] → gets hydroxylated again in kidney to 1,25-(OH)2 Vit D3 [*1,25-dihydroxyvitamin D3 or calcitriol*]
  - Active form is 1,25-dihydroxyvitamin D3
  - Lab test for Vit D deficiency is 25-hydroxyvitamin D3
- Vit D increases serum Ca^{2+} & phosphate while PTH (chief cells of parathyroid glands) increases Ca^{2+} & decreases phosphate

10.1.7 Limb development

- Limb buds are first seen at *8 weeks* of gestation
- Sonic hedge-hog (SHH) gene regulates limb bud formation / development
- Zone of polarizing activity (ZPA): controls AP axis (radioulnar axis, or thumb to small finger; great toe to small toe)
- Apical ectodermal ridge (AER): controls longitudinal limb growth
- Wnt controls dorsoventral axis

10.2 BONE

10.2.1 Bone formation

- Wolff law: bone remodels in response to mechanical stress applied to it

- Intramembranous: no cartilage model
    - Flat bones, physeal growth, primary bone healing (Haversian remodeling) with absolute stability
        - Primary bone healing: cutting cones, osteoclasts & osteoblasts remodel lamellar bone
    - Cleidocranial dysplasia: Cbfa1/Runx2 mutation leading to dysfunction of intramembranous ossification
- Endochondral: cartilage model
    - Long bones, secondary bone healing with relative stability
        - Secondary bone healing: callus formation

10.2.2 Bone morphogenetic protein (BMP)
- BMP binds to serine/threonine kinase receptor → SMAD signaling pathway
- BMPs induce host progenitor cell migration & differentiation at fracture site (*inflammatory stage* of fracture healing)
- BMP2: FDA-approved for acute open tibia fracture after IMN & ALIF
    - Best alternative to iliac crest autograft
    - BMP2 is involved in chondrogenic differentiation from mesenchymal cells
- BMPs 5, 6, 7 are involved in osteoinduction & osteogenesis
    - BMP7 is FDA-approved for long bone nonunion & posterolateral lumbar fusion
- BMP3 has no osteoinductive potential
- BMP is important in apoptosis of interdigital web spaces during development

10.2.3 Osteoclast
- Osteoclast is derived from monocyte/macrophage lineage (not mesenchymal stem cells)
- Interaction between osteoclast & osteoblast: when PTH binds to PTH receptor on osteoblast, osteoblast secretes RANKL → RANKL binds to RANK on osteoclast, leading to bone resorption
    - Osteoblast also secretes osteoprotegerin, which binds to RANKL & thus inhibits osteoclast activity
- Bone resorption at Howship's lacunae
    - Ruffled border of osteoclast attaches to bone surface: integrin on

osteoclast binds to vibronectin on bone surface
- Vibronectin contains Arg-Gly-Asp (RGD) sequence, which is an integrin recognition sequence
  - Carbonic anhydrase lowers pH of Howship's lacunae & cathepsin K breaks down organic bone matrix

10.2.4 Bone biology

- Compressive strength from proteoglycans & calcium hydroxyapatite $(Ca10(PO4)6(OH)2)$; tensile strength from type I collagen
- Circulation: periosteal arterioles supply outer third of diaphysis, nutrient artery supplies inner two-thirds (60% of cortical bone of a long bone)
  - Perichondrial artery supplies growth plate
- Bone graft substitutes

Cancellous chips	Osteoconductive
Demineralized bone matrix	Osteoconductive, osteoinductive

10.2.5 Nonunion

- Bone stimulator MOA: electrical stimulation → upregulation of TGF-β & BMPs
- NSAIDs block COX-1 and COX-2 which then decreases PG production → inhibits callus formation (secondary bone healing/endochondral ossification) via inhibiting chondrogenic differentiation

Atrophic	No biologic capacity to heal, no callus • Need mechanical stability & biology
Oligotrophic	Biologic capacity to heal, no ability to initiate healing, little callus
Hypertrophic	Biologic capacity to heal, abundant callus • Need mechanical stability

10.3 CARTILAGE

10.3.1 Growth plate

Zone	Importance	Relevance
Reserve		

Proliferative	Chondrocyte proliferation	Achondroplasia
Hypertrophic • Zone of maturation • Zone of degeneration • Zone of provisional calcification	Zone of provisional calcification: chondrocyte death, matrix calcification (Type X collagen is important)	Hypertrophic zone: • SCFE • Salter Harris fractures Zone of provisional calcification • Rickets

- Primary spongiosa (metaphysis): scurvy
- Groove of Ranvier: appositional growth of long bone

10.3.2 Articular cartilage
- Collagen restrains swelling pressure of aggrecan in articular cartilage
  - Type I collagen: bone, tendon, ligament, meniscus, fibrocartilage, annulus fibrosis
  - Type II collagen: articular cartilage, nucleus pulposus
- Superficial zone of articular cartilage has high collagen & low proteoglycan content
  - Chondrocytes are flat, collagen fibers oriented parallel to joint surface
  - Chondrocyte progenitor cells are in superficial zone
- Deep zone: chondrocytes are round, collagen fibers oriented perpendicular to joint surface
  - Highest proteoglycan content
- Tidemark separates articular cartilage from subchondral bone; articular cartilage only heals if injury crosses tidemark into subchondral bone
- With advanced age, articular cartilage becomes more brittle because of increased in glycation end products
  - Aging also leads to conversion of disc to fibrocartilage & an increase keratin sulfate to chondroitin sulfate ratio
- PTHrP is important in maintenance of articular cartilage phenotype during growth & development
- Synovium: *type B* cells produce synovial fluid
- Prolonged non-weight bearing results in cartilage thinning

10.3.3 Intervertebral disc
- Annulus fibrosus (type I collagen) is derived from mesoderm (i.e., sclerotomal cells); nucleus pulposus (type II collagen) is derived from notochord
- Nucleus pulposus (NP): highest proteoglycan content (low collagen : proteoglycan ratio)
  - With aging, size & cellularity of NP decrease; there is also loss of aggrecan
- Disc degeneration is associated with increased fibronectin fragmentation & proteoglycan fragmentation
  - Greatest risk factor for degeneration is genetics
  - Degeneration is associated with increase in collagen I & decrease in collage II
- Disc relies on endplate for metabolism (nutritional supply & waste removal)

10.4 MUSCLE, TENDON, LIGAMENT & NERVE

10.4.1 Muscle fibers
- Type I (slow twitch, red): type I fibers have low activation threshold & therefore are recruited first when muscle contracts
  - Aerobic / oxidative
- Type II (fast twitch, white): anaerobic / glycolytic
- Aerobic activity lasting <10 seconds: ATP, creatine phosphate
- Marathon runner (aerobic activity lasting longer than 4 minutes) gets muscle energy primarily from glycogen & fatty acids
- Sarcomere
  - A band: myosin filament
  - I band: actin-only
  - H zone: myosin-only
- Force is proportional to cross-sectional area of muscle
- Working out increases muscle mass via muscle fiber hypertrophy
- Contraction: isometric (same length), isotonic (same force), concentric (muscle shortens), eccentric (muscle lengthens), isokinetic (same velocity)

10.4.2 Tendon
- Decorin (a proteoglycan) controls tendon collagen fiber size during growth and repair after injury.
- Fibrillin is involved with elastin deposition w/in tendon—elastin responsible for tendon crimp
- Sheathed tendon receives nutrients via diffusion from synovial sheath
- Tendon repair is weakest at 7-10 days postoperative & strongest at 6 months postoperative
- Intrinsic tendon repair: slower healing but decreased adhesion formation (compared to extrinsic tendon repair)
- Golgi organs (provide steady state info during large stimulations for prolonged periods), Pacini corpuscles (sensitive, fast-acting mechanoreceptors), and Ruffini endings (sensitive but can relay info over prolonged periods like Golgi organs) are located at myotendinous junction
- Free nerve endings (nociception) are located in enthesis (bone-tendon junction)

10.4.3 Ligament
- Indirect insertion: ligament attaches to periosteum via Sharpey collagen fibers
- Direct insertion (4 transition zones): ligament → fibrocartilage → mineralized fibrocartilage → bone

10.4.4 Nerve injury

	Myelin	Axon	Endoneurium	Wallerian degeneration	Prognosis
Neurapraxia	Disrupted	Intact	Intact	No	Reversible
Axonotmesis	Disrupted	Disrupted	Intact	Yes	Reversible
Neurotmesis	Disrupted	Disrupted	Disrupted	Yes	Irreversible

- Radial nerve injury has best potential for recovery after graft repair
- Collagen conduit if defect <2.5 cm; autologous nerve graft if defect >2.5 cm

- Hierarchical structure of peripheral nerve (inside out): axon, myelin sheath, endoneurium, fascicles, perineurium, epineurium

10.5 MEDICATIONS

10.5.1 Anticoagulation

Medication	Mechanism of Action
Heparin / enoxaparin	ATIII activation • Reverse with protamine
Warfarin	Blocks vitamin K epoxide reductase → inhibits factors 2, 7, 9 & 10 • Reverse with vit K
Fondaparinux	Indirect Xa inhibitor
Aspirin	Inhibits thromboxane A2 (irreversible)
Rivaroxaban, apixaban	Direct Xa inhibitor (rapid onset, low potential for interaction w/ other drugs and foods, predictable AC effect, no monitoring needed; cost more than LMWH and Coumadin because newer)
Dabigatran, argatroban, —rudin	Direct thrombin (IIa) inhibitor

- LMWH (e.g., enoxaparin): highest risk of developing hematoma
- Unfractionated heparin & LMWH: heparin-induced *thrombocytopenia* (HIT)
- TXA (clotting promoter) inhibits plasminogen
- Hypercoagulability (thrombophilia)
  - Factor V Leiden: increased thrombin activation.
    - Has NOT been shown to portend increased risk of VTE post-operatively and thus no specific AC regimen or change in chemoprophylaxis warranted relative to other standard post-operative patients
  - Protein C or S deficiency
  - Surgery causes release of *thromboplastin* (tissue factor), thought to be responsible for higher DVT postoperative
    - Pulmonary embolism: most common presenting

symptom is *dyspnea*
- No specific AAOS guidelines on use of chemoprophylaxis in isolated lower extremity trauma in patients with no risk factors (smoker, prior DVT, obesity)—studies have shown equal rates of VTE in otherwise healthy patients with and without ppx
- Hemophilia A (factor 8 deficiency) & B (factor 9 deficiency): X- linked recessive.

10.5.2 Antibiotics
- Inhibit cell wall synthesis: penicillin, cephalosporins (cefazolin, cefepime, ceftriaxone), vancomycin, bacitracin
  - o Vancomycin inhibits crosslinking of peptidoglycans and binds directly to cell wall
  - o Cephalosporins bind to and inhibit PBP
    - MRSA: mecA gene encodes penicillin-binding protein (PBP), which is responsible for bacterial resistance to penicillin
- Inhibit protein synthesis: buy AT 30, CELl at 50
  - o Inhibit 30S: aminoglycosides (gentamicin, tobramycin), tetracyclines (doxycycline)
  - o Inhibit 50S: clindamycin, erythromycin (macrolides), linezolid
- Inhibit DNA synthesis: fluoroquinolones (ciprofloxacin), metronidazole
  - o Fluoroquinolones specifically inhibit DNA gyrase
- Inhibit RNA synthesis: rifampin
- Inhibit folate synthesis: TMP-SMX

10.5.3 Others

Medication	Mechanism of Action
Bupivacaine, lidocaine	Inhibit Na channel
Gabapentin	Binds presynaptic Ca channel & inhibits release of NTs
Acetaminophen	Inhibits PGE2 production through IL-1β

10.6 STATISTICS

10.6.1 Basic statistics

- Prevalence (total cases at a single time point) vs incidence (total new cases over a specific time period)
- Sensitivity: true positive / (true positive + false negative)
  - Best screening test has high sensitivity
  - SnNOut (high sensitivity, negative, rules out)
- Specificity: true negative / (true negative + false positive)
  - SpPIn (high specificity, positive, rules in)
- False positive rate: false positive / all patients without disease
- False negative rate: false negative / all patients with disease
- Positive predictive value: true positive / (true positive + false positive)
- Negative predictive value: true negative / (true negative + false negative)
- Number needed to treat: 1 / absolute risk reduction
- Type I (α) error: reject null hypothesis although it is true
- Type II (β) error: accept null hypothesis although it is false
- Power analysis to determine sample size needed for a study; perform power analysis to minimize type II (β) error
  - Power = $1 - \beta$
- Mann-Whitney U test: comparing 2 independent continuous variables in a *non-normal* distribution
- Chi-square: 2 categorical variables
- Student's t-test: 2 continuous variables (comparing means), *normal* distributions
- Analysis of variance (ANOVA): 3 or more continuous variables
- Funnel plot: detect bias in meta-analysis studies
- Receiver operating characteristic (ROC) curve determines accuracy of a test
  - The larger the area under ROC curve, the more reliable the test is
- Kaplan-Meier curve: survival probability (y axis) vs years (x axis)

10.6.2 Level of evidence

Level	Description
I	Well-designed RCT

II	Poorly designed RCT, prospective cohort
III	Retrospective cohort, case control
IV	Case series
V	Case report, expert opinion

- Level of evidence of a systematic review depends on quality of studies used in the meta-analysis

10.7 MATERIAL SCIENCE

10.7.1 Basics
- Stress: force (or load) / area
- Strain: Δ length / original length
- Elastic (reversible) deformation
  - Toe region: straightening of elastin fibers
  - Slope of stress-strain curve in elastic zone is Young's modulus of elasticity (stiffness)
    - Least to most stiff (lowest to highest modulus): cartilage → cancellous bone → polyethylene → PMMA → cortical bone → titanium → ceramic
      - Modulus of titanium (~100 MPa) is most similar to that of cortical bone

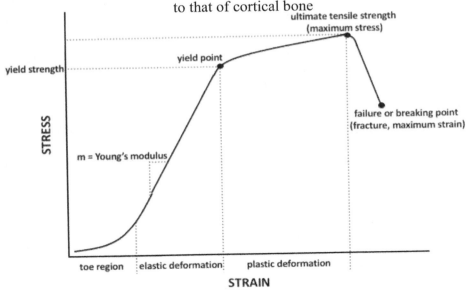

- Yield point is when elastic (reversible) deformation becomes plastic (irreversible) deformation
  - Yield strength: amount of stress to reach yield point
- Ultimate tensile strength: maximum stress before breaking
  - Fatigue failure: material fails below ultimate tensile strength due to repetitive loading
- Toughness: total energy per volume a material can absorb before fracturing
  - Area under stress-strain curve
- Brittle material (low toughness) vs ductile material (high toughness)
- Viscoelasticity: time-dependent stress-strain relationship
- Anisotropic material: mechanical properties depend on direction of applied force
- Creep: progressive deformation with a constant force applied over a period of time
- Load relaxation: over time, less stress is required to achieve same amount of elongation (strain)
- Bicortical screw has better torsional strength than unicortical screw
- PMMA: liquid monomer (monomethacrylate) which contains activator (N,N-Dimethyl-p-toluidine) added to polymer powder (polymethylmethacrylate) which contains initiator (benzoyl peroxide) → polymerization

10.7.2 Corrosion
- Galvanic corrosion: electrochemical gradient between two dissimilar metals
- Crevice (pitting) corrosion: formation of pits (fatigue cracks) due to oxygen tension.
  - Most susceptible to pitting are Austenitic stainless steel (A316L) and other primarily iron alloys
- Fretting corrosion: micromotion at junction of modular system.
- Resistant to corrosion are ceramics, Cobalt and Mo alloys as well as Ti alloys

10.8 CONDITIONS

10.8.1 Osteoporosis

- Peak bone mass is achieved during third decade of life; estrogen is most important hormone for peak bone mass
- WHO criteria: T score -1 to -2.5 is osteopenia; T score below -2.5 is osteoporosis
- Primary osteoporosis: missense mutation in LRP5 (LDL receptor-related protein 5); results in reduced signaling activity thru WNT pathway → decreased bone formation
- Fracture Risk Assessment Tool (FRAX) calculates 10-year risk for hip fracture
- Risk for future fragility fx is highest following vertebral compression fx
- Anabolic agent: PTH
    - o Has both *chondroprotective* and *chondroregenerative* properties in vivo
- Anti-resorptive agents: bisphosphonates, denosumab, estrogen, calcitonin, selective estrogen receptor modulators

Medication	Mechanism of Action
Bisphosphonates	Non-nitrogen containing: compete with ATP → apoptosis of osteoclasts Nitrogen containing: inhibit farnesyl pyrophosphate synthase in HMG-CoA reductase pathway Renal clearance: contraindicated in patients with severe CKD Side effects: jaw osteonecrosis, subtrochanteric fracture, esophagitis • Consider invasive dental work before initiating bisphosphonate therapy
Teriparatide (Forteo)	First 34 amino acids of PTH • Intermittent: bone formation • Continuous: bone resorption • Increases spinal fusion & fracture union rates

| Calcitonin | Intranasal spray
Inhibits sclerostin formation & inhibits osteoclast apoptosis |
| Denosumab | Monoclonal antibody that inhibits RANKL |

10.8.2 Rickets
- o Genu varum, physeal widening, metaphyseal cupping, rachitic rosary
- o Autosomal dominant hypophosphatemic rickets (FGF23 mutation.
  - o FGF23 acts on proximal tubules to increase phosphate excretion.
- o Nutritional rickets: vit D deficiency; osteomalacia in adults
  - o Oncogenic osteomalacia (tumor-induced): increased *FGF23* Activity
- o Vitamin D-dependent rickets
  - o Type I: mutation in renal 25-(OH) vitamin D-1α- hydroxylase
  - o Type II: mutation in receptor for 1,25(OH)2 vit D3
- o Vitamin D-resistant rickets (X-linked hypophosphatemic rickets)
  - o X-lined dominant: mutation in endopeptidase (phosphate-regulating neutral endopeptidase)
    - ▪ Impaired phosphate resorption by kidneys

10.8.3 Scurvy
- • Vit C deficiency → impaired collagen synthesis (i.e., hydroxylation)
- • Scurvy affects *primary spongiosa* of metaphysis

10.8.4 Paget's disease
- • Dysfunction of osteoclasts → increased bone resorption, focally increased skeletal remodeling
- • Associated with mutation in *sequestosome* gene
- • Juvenile Paget's disease (aka hereditary hyperphosphatasia) is caused by an inactivating mutation of OPG (gene: TNFRSF11B)
- • Administering pamidronate can minimize *EBL* for patients undergoing joint replacement
- • Paget's sarcoma: most common is osteosarcoma
- • Coarse trabeculae, cortical thickening
- • High bone turnover: elevated urinary hydroxyproline, N- & C-telopeptide

- Symptomatic: bisphosphonates
- No teriparatide since it increases risk of secondary osteosarcoma

10.8.5 Renal osteodystrophy
- Renal osteodystrophy leads to vit D deficiency → hypocalcemia
- Poor phosphate secretion → hyperphosphatemia
- Low Ca^{2+} & high phosphate → hyperparathyroidism (secondary hyperparathyroidism)

10.8.6 Hyperparathyroidism
- Primary (e.g., parathyroid adenoma): results in high Ca^{2+} & low phosphate
- Secondary (e.g., renal osteodystrophy): due to normal or low Ca^{2+} & high phosphate
- Brown tumor, osteitis fibrosa cystica

10.8.7 Crystal arthropathy
- Gout
  - Monosodium urate: needle-shaped crystals, *negatively* birefringent
  - Acute gout flare: indomethacin or colchicine
  - Chronic gout: allopurinol
  - Prophylaxis: colchicine
- Pseudogout (chondrocalcinosis): CCPD is rhomboid-shaped & *positively* birefringent

10.8.8 Osteomyelitis
- Bacteria form biofilm made of extracellular polymeric substances (EPS, or exopolysaccharide) such as glycocalyx (especially *Staphylococcus epidermidis*)
  - Bacteria in biofilm are in no-growth (*sessile*) phase → resistant to antibiotics
- Sequestrum (devitalized, necrotic bone), involucrum (new bone formation around sequestrum)
- *S. aureus* is most common in *all* patients

Newborn	Group B strep (e.g., *Streptococcus agalactiae*)
Sickle cell anemia (hemoglobin S)	Salmonella
Puncture wound through shoe	Pseudomonas

- Subacute osteomyelitis is Brodie abscess
- MRSA: Panton-Valentine leucocidin (PVL) cytotoxin causes injury to endothelium & therefore increases risk for DVT & septic emboli
- Marjolin's ulcer: malignant transformation of chronic draining sinus or wound bed/ulcer
  - Usually squamous cell carcinoma
- CRMO (chronic recurrent multifocal osteomyelitis): inflammatory bone process seen in kids—non-infectious so not treated w/ abx
  - Focal swelling, pain, and XR that mimic malignancy but w/out small round blue cells or any other malignant cells
  - Tx: Pamidronate

10.8.9 Septic arthritis

- *S. aureus* is most common in all patients.
  - Uses MSCRAMMS to bind to cell surfaces; induces IL-1 production and secretes exotoxins

Newborn	Group B strep (e.g., *Streptococcus agalactiae*)
Sexually active	*Neisseria gonorrhea* (gram negative diplococci)
Shoulder surgery, delayed presentation	*Propionibacterium acnes* (cultures must be held for at least 10 days)
IVDU	Pseudomonas
Cat or dog bite	Pasteurella
Human bite	Eikenella

- Aspirate: WBC >50,000 in native joint, >1,100 in prosthetic joint
  - N. gonorrhea usually induces a lower intraarticular WBC than S. aureus (< 50K)

- - Binds to cell surfaces via filamentous outer membranes
  - Also induces IL-1 production and direct cell damage via exotoxins
- Pediatric
  - Kocher criteria: (1) weight bearing, (2) T 38.5°C / 101.3°F, (3) ESR >40, (4) WBC >12,000
    - Predicated probability: 3 of 4 criteria (93.1%); 4 of 4 criteria (99.6%)
  - Transient synovitis: recent URI, no fevers/chills/general malaise, normal WBC/ESR/CRP
    - NSAIDs & observation
- Septic hip: FABER position because of lowest intracapsular hip pressure
  - Matrix metalloproteinases (MMPs) destroy articular cartilage
- Metaphyseal osteomyelitis can directly spread to cause septic arthritis in hip, shoulder, ankle & elbow joints but not knee; metaphysis of knee is extraarticular

10.8.10 Necrotizing fasciitis
- Diabetic is a major risk factor
- Usually polymicrobial; the most common organism is group A β-hemolytic strep

10.8.11 Miscellaneous
- FGFR2 important in bone growth, particularly embryonic development of bone in head/hands/feet
  - Mutations result in craniosynostoses (premature closure of bones in skull: Apert, Crouzon, Pfeiffer syndromes)
- FGF18 promotes chondrocyte proliferation via PI3K-AKT.
  - FGF18 attenuates cartilage degradation, increases Type 2 collagen deposition, and suppresses MMP13

DOMAIN 11: PRACTICE MANAGEMENT

11.1 BILLING
- New vs established patient: new patient defined as patient who has not been seen by treating provider or any other providers in same group / specialty within past 3 years
- Billing level is the *lowest* level of the 3 key components: history, examination & medical decision making
    - Need all 3 components in order to bill: history, exam & medical decision making
- Need all of the following to bill for consultation: requested by another physician, request is documented, patient's visit & consultant's opinions are documented, opinion is communicated back to requesting physician
    - Cannot bill for consultation if there is an expectation for transfer of care to you (treating provider)
- If already billed for fracture care (regardless of whether reduction was performed in clinic or in OR), all services related to treatment within 90 days is considered in global fee → cannot bill for visits or services during this time
    - Exception: application of splint or cast during global period is separately billable
- Modifier 25: **significant**, separately **identifiable** evaluation and management service by **same** physician on **same** day of procedure or other service
- Modifier 58: appended to second procedure (staged or related procedure) during global period

11.2 MISCELLANEOUS
- Consent is best obtained in clinic a few days before date of surgery
- Communication is key in preventing medical errors & lawsuits
- Illegal to alter medical record
- Physician Payments Sunshine Act: must report payments of >$10
- 4 legal elements of medical negligence: (1) duty, (2) breach of duty, (3) causation, (4) damages

- Workers' compensation case can be settled once patient has reached maximum medical improvement (MMI)
- Stark Law prohibits any provider from referring Medicare or Medicaid patients to a facility in which the provider has a financial relationship with
- A formal written complaint from a patient requires a formal response letter from provider
- In general, physicians are mandated to report child & elderly abuse but not spousal or intimate partner abuse
- Ethically but now lawfully required to inform patient of another physician's error
- Federal Trade Commission prohibits false advertising
- Termination of care: notify patient in writing, give an appropriate period of time before termination, be available to provider care during that time
- 3T MRI has *9x* proton energy of a 1.5T

11.2.1 2014 OITE
- Munchausen syndrome is facilitated by biologic mother who has knowledge of medicine
- Always use a certified interpreter
- IMN of closed tibial shaft fracture: stainless steel nail is associated with increased risk for adverse events (e.g., nonunion, revision, fracture of implant)
    o Because stainless steel nail causes more autodynamization (screw breakage)
- WBAT is not safe after ORIF of both bone forearm fracture
- There is a 40% actual lifetime intimate partner violence (IPV) among female patients at fracture clinics but only 10% surgeon- perceived IPV prevalence
    o Predictor of IPV: repeated ED visits
- Timed Up & Go test predicts functional outcome (e.g., need for walking aid) after hip hemiarthroplasty
- Occult hip fracture: if CT scan is negative & unable to obtain MRI (e.g., pacemaker), then obtain bone scan 72 hours after initial injury

- Lipid (20% fat) emulsion to reverse bupivacaine-related cardiac arrest (asystole from injecting bupivacaine into femoral vein)
- Sheathed tendons receive blood supply from vincula
- Tibialis anterior rupture: primary tendon repair & possible graft augmentation (e.g., with EHL transfer)
  - Consider gastrocnemius recession if there is contracture because it can compromise repair

11.2.2 2015 OITE

- Normal walking age is 12-18 months
- Scapular fracture is most commonly associated with concomitant chest injury
- Hip fracture: in-hospital mortality of 6%, 1-year mortality of 30%
  - Better outcomes if surgery within 48 hours
- Distal radius fracture: best reduction requires traction & volar translation of lunate
- Outpatient upper extremity surgery should go home with only 10 narcotic pills
- Elite adult athlete with avulsion of proximal hamstring insertion
  - Chronic → open debridement & repair

11.2.3 2016 OITE

- Frozen allograft has greater torsional & bending strength compared to freeze-dried allograft
  - Fresh allograft has highest immunogenicity
- Free nerve endings exist at bone-tendon junction → nociception
- Titanium has highest rate of bacterial adherence
- Adductor canal blockage for TKR blocks saphenous sensory but not femoral motor nerve function
- Pediatric distal tibia physeal fracture: physeal gap >3mm postreduction is predictor of premature physeal closure
- Patellar tendonitis (jumper's knee): stronger risk factor is hamstring / quadriceps inflexibility

11.2.4 2017 OITE
- Osteoblasts regulate hematopoietic cells & immune response via PTH-Jagged1-Notch pathway
  - PTH induces Jagged1 on osteoblasts; Jagged1 stimulates Notch receptors on hematopoietic stem cells, leading to cell proliferation
- EDC tendon laceration: after primary repair, use a yoke splint (relative motion splint) that holds MCPJ in slight extension but allows active ROM of DIP/PIP joints
- Chronic SPN nerve pain: neurotomy with transposition into bone
- During fracture healing, matrix metallopeptidase 13 (MMP-13) degrades cartilaginous extracellular matrix
- Tobacco use: conitine level (metabolite of tobacco) before surgery
- Disease-specific surgical outcome measure: neck disability index (NDI) for cervical spine pathology; Oswestry disability index (ODI) for lumbar spine pathology
- Tooth avulsion: rinse in water or saline & place in milk, saliva or sterile saline
- Pregnant patient: left lateral decubitus to minimize positional hypotension due to aortocaval compression
- Malignant hyperthermia: autosomal dominant
- Hypersensitivity to implant is type IV hypersensitivity: delayed, T cell mediated

11.2.5 2018 OITE
- Osteopoikilosis: AD inheritance, hundreds of *bone islands* usually centered around joints
  - Benign, usually asymptomatic → observation
- Loss of reduction of *volar ulnar rim* leads to volar translation of carpus after DRF
  - During ORIF, need to support lunate facet to prevent volar subluxation of carpus
- Supplemental immobilization is often required after flexible nailing of femoral or tibial shaft fracture

- D-zone test: determine whether *S. aureus* infections resistant to erythromycin are also resistant to clindamycin (inducible resistance)
- AVN of talus requiring TTC fusion: best approach is *lateral transfibular* approach
  - Allow removal of talus, preparation of tibiotalar & subtalar joints, and bone grafting
- Formal preoperative "time out" addresses problems associated with *variations in workflow patterns* among surgical team members
- Motor evoke potentials (MEPs): stimulation of motor cortex to corticospinal tract → spinal cord interneurons → anterior horn cells → peripheral nerve → skeletal muscle in an *efferent* direction
  - Sensory evoke potentials (SEPs): *afferent* direction; signal initiation in upper & lower extremities → transcranial recording of somatosensory cortex
- Groin flap: risk for injury to LFCN
- Osteoporosis unresponsive to long term bisphosphonate (antiresorptive) therapy: add teriparatide (anabolic)
- Most doctors interrupt patients within 23 seconds
- Hypothermia has not been shown to improve outcomes after SCI
- Isolated metastatic RCC to proximal femur: wide resection & proximal femoral replacement improves survival compared to CMN prophylactic fixation (higher rate of revision surgery)
- Pressure = force / area
  - Contact pressure is decreased by decreasing joint reactive forces & increasing contact area
- PROMIS: computer-adaptive test that minimizes floor & ceiling effects
- For tibial shaft fractures, suprapatellar nailing improves alignment compared to infrapatellar nailing
- Process improvement: retrospective review of cases for quality improvement (not considered research)
- Nonoperative 5th metacarpal fracture: *one visit* to evaluate & manage fracture with taping or splint & *optional* follow-up
- Distal radial physeal injury (gymnast's wrist): injury to *zone of provisional calcification*

- Mycobacterium marinum: fishing- or water-related injuries
  - Incubation of culture at 2 temperatures: 35° C & 28 to 32° C
- Front passenger seat: airbag should be turned off for children <80 lbs
- Best randomization: computer randomization with assignments placed into sealed envelopes
- Initial step in applying evidence-based medicine (EBM) is formulating a specific clinical question

11.2.6 2019 OITE

- Transient osteoporosis of hip: atraumatic, happens in middle-aged men & pregnant females
  - MRI: homogenous pattern of edema of femoral head/neck; low-intensity on T1, high-intensity on T.
  - Tx: PWB
- Blood supply to skin paddle for latissimus dorsi myocutaneous flap is thoracodorsal artery
- Following fragility fx, referral to bone density education & treatment program ("fracture liason" program) has greatest impact on prevention of future fragility fx
- Shelf life of freeze-dried bone is 5+ years
- *Short term relationship* is associated w/ increased risk of IPV
- Level 1 studies require >80% follow-up; otherwise they are level 2 (even if double-blinded RCTs)
- CDC defines "exposure-prone" procedures as insertion of a needle tip into a body cavity or simultaneous presence of a healthcare worker's finger and a needle or other sharp object in a highly confined anatomic site. If surgeon tests positive for HIV then he/she must notify patient when *scheduling for exposure-prone procedure*
- Per IRS, independent contractor is defined when the employer determines or controls the result of the work performed and not the methods or means of accomplishing the result

11.2.7 2020 OITE

- Coccidioidomycosis (aka "Valley Fever"): soil-borne fungal infection in SW USA and Latin America
  - Most patients are asymptomatic but <1% develop hematogenous

seeding of bone, skin, soft tissue
- o Most common presentation complaint is bone pain
- o MRI w/ foci of increased T2 signal w/ sclerotic margins
- o Tx: debridement + antifungals
- Sports-related hematuria often occurs after strenuous exercise and is unrelated to NSAID use. Exercise is most likely cause of hematuria when remainder of examination is unremarkable.
  - o Stop exercise for 48 to 72 hours & repeat urinalysis. Further work-up is necessary if hematuria persists
- Obesity, OCP use, and GI +/- renal issues increase risk of DVT in elective surgery population
  - o Consider Hematology consult preop
- Mycobacterium marinum, grows best in Löwenstein-Jensen medium at 30°C. Mycobacterium tuberculosis also grows in Löwenstein-Jensen but at core temperature of 37°C.
  - o Thayer-Martin medium is for Neisseria gonorrhoeae, which more often presents clinically as a migratory arthritis in sexually active individuals
- IV/topical fluconazole is most effective against Candida PJIs
- Exercise-induced bronchospasm: short-acting beta-2 agonist
- Septal hematoma is emergency in child—treat w/ urgent decompression w/ needle or incision and drainage w/ packing; delayed treatment can cause saddle-nose deformity due to ischemic cartilage loss
- Auricular hematoma occurs b/w perichondrium and auricular cartilage and if not decompressed urgently can result in avascular necrosis of cartilage → "cauliflower ear"
- Hypoprolactinemic amenorrhea: part of female athlete triad (low energy availability—w/ or w/out eating disorder, hypoprolactinemic amenorrhea, reduced BMD)
- Waddell signs: non-organic/non-anatomic pain; associated w/ malingering
- Lyme disease testing: screen w/ ELISA (sensitive but not specific); if positive or indeterminate, confirm w/ Western Blot (specific of Lyme antibodies)
- Circular frame: orthogonally tensioned wires vs half-pins
  - o Half pins w/ decreased axial compression and increased

transverse shear
- When harvesting mesenchymal stems cells from iliac crest, use *posterior* aspiration w/ *multiple smaller volumes* for maximum yield
- Most common reason for litigation following THA: *nerve injury (38%)* > LLD (26%) > infection (22%)
- 45-55% burnout rate for US physicians